But Not FORSAKEN

By
HELEN GOOD BRENNEMAN

Christian Light Publications, Inc.
Harrisonburg, Virginia 22802

BUT NOT FORSAKEN

Christian Light Publications, Inc., Harrisonburg, Virginia 22802
© 1983 by Christian Light Publications, Inc.
All rights reserved. Published 1983
Printed in the United States of America

12 11 10 09 08 07 06 05 04 03   9 8 7 6 5

Cover Art: Anna Mae Pellman

ISBN 0-87813-954-0

THE REFUGEE

A victim of a "righteous war,"
Her deep-lined face, her aged heart sore
With thinking of her loved ones—
Her starving, freezing, dying sons.
    For only souls like she
    Know what it means to be
    A weary refugee.

Yet midst the nothing that she owned
I saw her standing there enthroned
In regal garments—serene mind,
Painless memories now enshrined
    In gold, and faith that He
    Who rules eternity
    Does love a refugee!

Lord, in these days of disarray
I feel constrained to ask today—
If everything I know or own
Should in a violent blast be blown
    To bits, help me to be
    In sweet humility
    Like this poor refugee.

—HELEN GOOD BRENNEMAN

PREFACE

IT WAS IN THE YEARS 1947-48 that my husband and I had the privilege of serving the Mennonite Central Committee refugee camp in Gronau, Germany. The camp, which began as a small emergency measure, grew in size to a large, bustling community and emigration center, usually housing 700 or 800 people, sometimes bulging its walls to accommodate as many as 2,000 homeless transitees.

Should anyone endeavor to collect all the stories which these brethren-in-need brought with them from their homeland and their long, arduous trek, the collection would fill many volumes with fascinating tales of pathos and adventure. The family which arrived intact, mother, father, and all the children together, was rare indeed. Every individual had a history of hardships and severe trials, and each person living in camp had his own moments of fear and anxiety over the past, present, and future.

Yet despite all the difficulties of a refugee existence, God had not forgotten His people nor had His people forgotten Him. From the debris of shattered hopes and dreams rose a monumental faith in God that amazed those of us who had never experienced such unfortunate circumstances. At times we witnessed answers to prayer which were nothing short of modern-day miracles and which strengthened our own faith.

When we had said good-bye to these people who had taught us so much, when the last hand had clasped ours and the last "God bless you" was still ringing in our ears, we realized that we could never be the same people we had been before, that we could never again take for granted the blessings of one another, of home, of food, of material comfort, of spiritual nourishment. The lesson the refugees had taught us burned within us and demanded to be told. And the more we told the story of the refugees, the more we were convinced that it was ours to share.

Out of this conviction comes *But Not Forsaken*, the refugee story in narrative form—fiction, yet not fiction, for it is based upon many real-life tales related to us by refugee friends. Maria Penner's border crossing, for instance, is almost exactly as a refugee woman recalled her experience, except that her account was even more amazing. God helped her pass *six* guards on the Russian Zonal border. MCC workers witnessed a number of dramatic reunions between members of families who for years believed one another to be dead.

My hope is that this book will create a greater understanding and deeper sympathy for the many homeless wanderers in our world today.

May, 1954
Iowa City, Iowa

HELEN GOOD BRENNEMAN

INTRODUCTION

Unless you have personally experienced the trauma and heartache of being cruelly separated from those you love most dearly, you may find it difficult to really identify with those suffering from the ravages of war and religious persecution. In *But Not Forsaken* you will find yourself in their midst sharing their trials, their sorrows, and their joys.

Here is a gripping account depicting the tragedy and triumph of those forced to forsake their earthly possessions, only to find that God would never forsake them. Here, too, family life is depicted in the pathos of painful separation and the rapture of reunion. Here you will read of those whose faith was sorely tried but who were not forsaken.

You will observe that we have reprinted this book originally produced by another publisher. We at Christian Light feel it must be kept in circulation, despite the fact that we cannot endorse such things as Christmas trees, plays (drama), or the wearing of costumes.

Whatever your present family relationships, this compelling portrayal of family loyalty calls one to a deeper appreciation for blessings too often taken for granted. Once more we present these pages, confident that they will strengthen your faith in the unswerving faithfulness of Him who has promised never to leave nor to forsake those who put their trust in Him.

Christian Light Publications

1

*"Segne Vater, diese Speise,
    Uns zur Kraft, und Dir zum Preise."**

MARIA PENNER kept her head bowed for several moments after the children had finished returning thanks, then raised her eyes and smiled at Hans, sitting across the table from her. Thanking God just for the food somehow never seemed enough, for Hans and the little ones were seated safely around her. Only baby Lenie, quietly sleeping on her cot in the corner, was missing from Maria's family circle. Slowly she rose and walked over to the stove to get the soup, noting out of the corner of her eye that Hans had busied himself with slicing the thick, black bread.

"I visited Frau Schmidt and her mother again for a little while this afternoon, Hans."

Maria was back at the table pouring the hot liquid into the tin containers. "It seems as though even an hour with her makes me feel—well—better, somehow."

"Frau Schmidt let Mamma borrow her Bible for a while." Rosie had obviously been impressed. Her pale, freckled face leaned forward eagerly to give this bit of information, one auburn braid dangling nervously over the back of her chair, the other peeping curiously around her head.

*Free translation:
    "Heavenly Father, bless this food,
      For Thy praise, and for our good."

"And Papa, Mamma read us some stories, Rosie and me."

Hansie paused only for a moment between gulps to add this morsel of news, but Maria couldn't find it in her heart to rebuke him for his greediness this evening. All afternoon he had complained of being hungry and had inquired periodically *when* supper would be ready. One of the hardest trials for the refugee mother was knowing that her children never had their hunger truly satisfied. Hansie's small, tousled crown was propped by a spindly elbow, as though he were almost too tired to hold it up. With his other hand he hurriedly scooped in the thin soup.

"Hans, the soup will last longer if you don't eat it quite so fast." Big Hans leaned over the boy diplomatically, and laid a firm hand on his narrow shoulders.

How good, Maria thought, to see the two together! But the lines of concern in Hans' tired face deepened as he turned and looked at her.

"Do you think you should read the Bible to the children, Maria? We are still in Russian-occupied territory. I can't help thinking we are still being watched. They're always around somewhere and—children talk—"

A warning glance from his wife halted Hans in his remarks. Suddenly he remembered the nightmares Rosie had been having again, just when they were getting her emotionally settled, nightmares of frightening faces peering in the window, of large, grotesque, uniformed figures grabbing from the shadows. She had grown so afraid of the dark that the slightest implication of danger made her almost hysterical. Instead of voicing aloud their increasing fear of being sent back to their Russian homeland, Maria and Hans had recently begun whispering together at night when the little ones were asleep, talking out their problems as they huddled close on their hard bed in the corner.

Yes, Rosie had stopped eating; she was staring at her spoon with a troubled look.

"Rosie," Hans breathed her name softly. "Rosie, I didn't mean to frighten you, only to remind you that we don't tell our friends at school what we do and talk about at home. It—it isn't safe."

He looked helplessly for moral support at the tall, dark-haired woman who stood earnestly intent, the battered soup pan frozen in mid-air. Getting no encouragement, he cleared his throat, finishing awkwardly.

"It's just nobody's business what we say here at home."

"Oh, Papa, you've told us that so often! We don't tell things, especially about the Bible, at school, though I know Hilda and Retha have Bibles and they don't always have to be so afraid. I don't know what to talk about any more to them, I'm so afraid I'll say something I shouldn't."

"Can't you just play and sing the folk games with the other children and talk about your studies?" It seemed logical to Hans' grown-up mind, and he was ready to end the conversation.

"But, Papa, the Bible says not to tell lies, and yet we almost have to lie about the Bible. And another thing, Hilda keeps asking me where I'm from, and where I was born, and when I don't answer her, she bothers me nearly to death until the bell rings for class. I feel like making up a place, but Mamma says it's wrong to say something that isn't true."

11

Since Rosie knew from past experience that her parents had no answer for this question, she returned to her soup, which was now getting cold.

Hans and Maria did not like to argue in front of the children. Looking at Hans, Maria knew what he was thinking, that in the frightful years in postwar Germany expediency had to take the place of conviction; religion with its beautiful ideology had failed. He would have told the children a plausible story to give their friends, if he hadn't known how much that would hurt her, how contradictory that would be to the teaching she gave them every day. It was the only flaw in their complete marital happiness, his reasoning versus her faith, but it popped up at every important junction of their path.

"I wish we could take the children out of school until we can go westward again."

She purposely ignored the woebegone expressions this suggestion brought to the faces of both her offspring. They had spent too much time out of school already. At every new home along their trek from Russia to the East Zone of Germany, they had had to start all over, making friends, avoiding answers to curious questions with the simple statement, "We have no home; we are just refugees."

Though there were many others like them, there were always persistent children at school, who, either for friendliness or sheer mischief, would delve into their well-guarded past. And then, just as they had earned a nice set of friends, had inspired the confidence and respect of their teachers, and were making real progress in their studies, they were rooted out of that academic soil and transplanted into a new and hostile one.

"Oh, well!" Hansie imitated the posture Big Hans took when he was philosophizing. "I'll be glad when we leave that old school."

"Why?" Regardless of their differences in spiritual things, Maria and Hans always came together in their concern for their children.

"I don't like the boys at school."

"Why, Hansie, you have never had trouble getting along with other people." Maria gazed at the wise, sad young face resting in grimy hands, one eyebrow lifted. How like a little old man he sat there, hunched up on the edge of his seat!

"Because—because they don't like me."

"Don't like you? Why?" This from Maria.

"They make fun of me—say I'm just a no-good refugee, and tease me about—oh, never mind."

If there was anything Hansie didn't like to show in his stubborn young make-up, it was weakness. He jumped up from the table so quickly that everyone stared at him in surprise as he dashed over to the rumpled pile of ragged covers which made his bed. Throwing himself down on his face, he held back the tears.

Hans pushed his chair away from the table and hurried over to the boy, knowing that his children were not accustomed to throwing tantrums. Surely this was a real issue in the life of his son.

"Come on, boy, face it," he advised evenly. "We men look at our problems straight and go on from there." How he wished, even as he said it, that he were telling the truth. Little Hans sat up with a jerk.

"It isn't anything." Since the silence that met this reply

13

showed that no one believed him, Hansie swallowed hard, stuck his feet under him, and finished.

"It's my shoes they tease me so much about. Not that they have such good ones. Some of the poorer children even wear *Klompen* to school, but mine are so much too big. The other fellows trip me when I walk by their desks."

"Do they tease you about your other clothes?"

Hansie glanced down at his patched shirt and baggy trousers with the frayed pockets. "They all have to wear patches. They don't notice that so much."

"Let me see your shoes. Stand up."

Carefully Hans inspected the length of the boy's feet and the length of the shoes. He had been so grateful when Waldemar had given them to him, though it made his heart ache to think of the circumstances. He had gone to the factory as usual that morning and had met his friend Waldemar coming around the corner of the hall, his shoulders bent, his lips pale, his hair uncombed.

"The boy is gone," his friend had murmured. Then after several minutes in which Hans had laid his hand on Waldemar's shoulder and they had both stared at the floor, Waldemar had handed him the shoes.

"Give them to your boy. It's all Claus had worth passing on."

But they hadn't really fit; they had made Hansie twice as clumsy as his ordinary boy awkwardness. Yet they were such good shoes, with at least another six months' wear.

"They're not large enough for Mamma, are they?" Big Hans inquired now, caressing them in his hand as he pretended to examine them.

Maria glanced sympathetically at her son.

14

"They're several sizes too small for me, and Hansie had completely worn out his other pair. Do you remember, Hansie, how we thanked God that He had sent you another pair of shoes? The baby used up our last coupon and we had no more marks. If you can just get along a little while, maybe the Lord will provide us with a pair that will fit better."

Big Hans returned to his supper, seeing that Hansie realized the futility in further complaint about the shoes.

"Come on, Hansie, and eat this other piece of bread." Maria spoke in a whisper, her low voice softened by love and pity. "I'm not hungry this evening."

She avoided her husband's eyes, knowing what they would be saying, how they would accuse her of "righteous" deceit in pretending not to be hungry for the sake of her boy.

There was a sudden knock on the door to the adjoining room, and in answer to Hans' "Yes," Frau Friesen entered, a little reluctantly when she noticed that the family was still eating.

"*Guten Appetit,*" she said dutifully, seating her tall, gangly frame on the pile of blankets in the corner. Leaning with studied effort over a thick, dark stocking, she worked nervously to add another patch to an almost ridiculous mass of confusion.

"Tante Anni, have you had supper already? Won't you drink a cup of coffee with us?" Maria would sacrifice her last crust before she would eat without sharing with her good friend Anni. Before she offered it, she had already rinsed her own cup briefly, refilling it with the hot, artificial wartime brew the Germans flattered with the name "coffee."

15

"Oh, but you shouldn't. I—I had supper and—uh—washed my dishes. I craved only a little company."

Frau Friesen, aware that her apologies were both unnecessary and unnatural (for she spent many happy hours with the Penners), laid the stocking on her lap, took the proffered cup, and ventured a smile that was as far from the real thing as the "coffee" she sipped so slowly and abstractedly. That something was on her mind was clear to Maria, who read trouble and fear on the face of her usually cheerful friend.

"Rosie, you and Hansie wash the dishes quickly so you can get plenty of sleep for school tomorrow. But be careful not to wake Lenie."

"How is the baby?"

"Frankly, I'm worried, Anni. She's been sleeping well for the past few hours, but she has seemed feverish all day, turning and tossing in her sleep. The room is so dark except by the window. I had her lying there most of the day."

Maria looked around at the dismal room, reviewing afresh the cracks in the plaster, the broken window glass that they had stuffed with cardboard, the crude table which served so many purposes. Yet, on their long trek westward, there had been much worse rooms. There had been the one in Poland with the dirt floor and the rats. And, later, there had been the smelly lean-to against an old barn which they had called home when they first arrived in the East Zone of Germany. Indeed, many times the out-of-doors had been their only shelter, the heaven a distant ceiling, their only furniture ragged covers for a bed and a makeshift stove of rubble.

Hans was kneeling beside his youngest, his good face

16

lined with concern. Maria slipped over to his side and laid her experienced hand on the forehead of their child.

"Hans, I think Lenie's better. She isn't so hot and doesn't cry out in her sleep anymore!" She whispered it, but her words came forth with such staccato excitement that the child opened her eyes, looking from one parent to the other.

"I'm thirsty."

"Oh, praise the Lord, I know the child's better."

Maria quickly took a cup from the table, filling it with water. Then she lifted it to the lips of little Lenie. After a few grateful swallows, Lenie fell into another heavy sleep. How much Maria wished they could find a doctor who would be willing to come to their aid! But doctors were few in comparison to the overwhelming need.

When Big Hans had laid out the blankets on the floor and had heard Hansie's and Rosie's prayers, both of which terminated in the plea, "and please make Lenie well," he walked slowly over to Anni and Maria, pulling a chair up beside his wife. The word "Russian" had caught his attention and given him misgivings. Warily he glanced over at the pyramid of covers in the corner and felt reassured that the children, tired from a strenuous day, had dropped off to sleep. He was glad that the women were whispering, for the thought of another session of comforting nervous little Rosie was most disturbing. Secretly he determined once more to make definite plans to go westward again, westward toward freedom from the fear and want that constantly haunted their very existence.

2

THERE WERE TEARS in Maria's voice. "But, Anni, are you sure? Hans, listen to what Anni is saying." She grasped his hand and he noticed that hers was damp, the muscles tense. "Start all over, Anni."

Anni Friesen, still seated on the heap that would eventually be Hans' and Maria's bed, looked up at the two figures leaning intently toward her. The gathering dusk almost concealed the expressions on their faces, but the tension that gripped them could have been felt in the dark.

"I was coming home from the factory this evening, just before I came into your room. I lied, please forgive, I lied when I said I had supper. I couldn't eat a bite. Just when I turned the corner down on Felderstrasse I bumped head on into a soldier. We didn't either of us see the other until we had collided."

She paused and shuddered, then continued breathlessly.

"If it had been a German soldier, I would have begged his pardon and gone on. But he was Russian—the sheepskin cap, the leather jacket, the blue-gray uniform. There wasn't any doubt about it, I tell you. I just stood there trembling from head to toe. I know he was suspicious. He demanded my identification. He asked me where I was from. I said this was my home town. I showed him my papers. He—he paid special attention to my present address, and—"

She had been speaking fast and dramatically in *Plattdeutsch*, and now burst into tears. It was not necessary to say more. Maria, on the floor beside her, was weeping in sympathy and mutual fear. Hans had buried his face in his hands, thinking, thinking.

Was it all her imagination? In Maria's blind loyalty to her friend Anni, she would not look at things objectively. He, as the man of the family, would have to weigh the evidences and decide if Anni's fears were justified. Hans had had experience before with women whose nerves were war-shattered and who would become hysterical at the least alarm, but he had to admit that this was not Tante Anni, regardless of her terrible past. He had seen many men who were not made of the courageous stuff that composed her solid frame.

"But many of the German populace around us are also afraid of *them*," Hans thought aloud. "They would have reacted in much the same way. Did he try speaking Russian to you? Tante Anni, did he hint that he suspected where you're from?"

His voice was suddenly demanding, and for a moment the woman before them stopped to think, closing her eyes as though by that gesture she could exclude the nonessential details of the soldier's appearance, breaking the awful silence with occasional sobs.

"It happened so quickly. Now that I think of it, he gave no real indication of knowing. But who can guess what is in *their* minds?"

"Then, Anni, I think you had better get your rest and think no more of it. After the baby is well, we had better all move on again, even into the Western Zone, but I sort of hate the thought of trying to find another room, an-

19

other job, in another city. This room is miserable enough, but at least it has a ceiling and four walls, and you, Anni, have a room to yourself. I still don't know how you did that."

He grinned at her mischievously, relieving the tension by a fleeting smile.

Frau Friesen, unaware of his inner doubts, felt quieted by the firm and matter-of-fact reasoning of the man. Sometimes Hans reminded her of her own husband, missing since 1941 when he, along with many other Mennonite men and boys from the Ukraine, had been drafted into forced labor in Siberia. How often when she watched the reunited Hans and Maria, she thought of her own beloved Gerhardt. How often in the lonely hours across the wall from the Penners she wondered if Gerhardt lived, and what conditions he and the many thousands of other *verschleppt* Mennonites were enduring. She loved to dream that he lay at her side, that he comforted her when she was frightened, that he took her in his arms as of old. Yet through the daytime hours she managed to put on a courageous front as she worked at the mill.

"Life as a refugee would not be so hard," she whispered after a long silence, "if it were not for the memories of the past and the fear of the future."

Maria looked out the window at the unlit streets below, then at the stars above the city, above the world with its maze of wars and man-made problems.

"And life as a refugee would not be endurable," she replied, "if it were not for beautiful memories of the past and hope for the future in Christ. Today Frau Schmidt lent me her Bible for a little while. I started to tell you about it, Hans."

She paused a moment, remembering that he had not wholeheartedly approved.

"It was such a thrill to leaf through it and read favorite verses after not having owned a Bible for all these years. I read some stories to the children about the Lord Jesus and how He healed the sick, and then suddenly I saw a verse which Frau Schmidt had underlined in red. I copied it."

Hans and Anni watched the dim figure hurry over to the bundle, ever packed and ready for quick flight, pulling from its folds a tiny slip of soiled paper. Catching the feeble light from the window, she leaned over her treasure with the eagerness of a scientist over a precious test tube, or like a hungry child over a bowl of good, hot soup. With all the expression, all the reverence her voice could command, she read the verses from the fourth chapter of II Corinthians, the ones which had meant so much to her as she read them from Frau Schmidt's Bible.

"We are troubled on every side, yet not distressed; we are perplexed, but not in despair; persecuted, but not forsaken; cast down, but not destroyed; always bearing about in the body the dying of the Lord Jesus, that the life also of Jesus might be made manifest in our body."

The silence that followed was somewhat awkward. Maria sat down again at Hans' side, laying her hand on his and feeling the length of his fingers and the hardness of his knuckles, knowing his love. She wondered if he took any stock in what she was saying. Had the words of the Holy Bible helped Anni as they had helped her? To gether they sat staring out the window at the stars, enjoying the privacy of their own thoughts.

"Beautiful memories," Anni repeated as if to herself, "hope for the future. Yes, Maria, my hope for the future is pretty dim sometimes, but the memories are so clear. Every night he is with me like your Hans is with you, hearing my troubles and my hopes and saying the comforting little things he used to say when we were together. We were *so* happy."

Again Anni began weeping unashamedly, Maria with her. She seldom cried, especially in their presence. Certainly Tante Anni was upset tonight.

Hans rose uneasily from his chair, releasing his hand from Maria's, and walked over to the window. Facing the grim realities of their life as refugees, enduring the miseries of postwar life, and trying at the same time to shake off the most diabolical of memories, what could a man do to preserve his sanity? He could not weep like a woman, letting out the pent-up tension and frustration in that way. He could not pray, for his idea of God was a God of order, a God of love, controlling the interests of men. Could there be such a God in this world of hungry children, in this world of hate and animal-like injustices? He could not accept the religious faith of his ancestors. For him there remained only one emotion— at least when he was stirred by the complete wretchedness and meaninglessness of life—fierce hatred for the oppressors.

Closing his fists tightly, he was for a moment his own god, justly avenging the blood of thousands of his brethren who had been murdered savagely; he was demanding justice for the tears of the multitudes of innocent women who had been torn from their husbands. How many "widows" there were who, like Anni, sat weeping, wondering whether their husbands were dead or whether they were bent under the tyranny of endless labor, unrewarded.

The Mennonites of Russia were part of a large group of German-speaking peoples who, by invitation of Catherine II of Russia, had settled the beautiful Ukraine. They had retained their own German culture within the Russian environment about them. Indeed, they had thrived in the Ukraine until the Bolshevik Revolution began a long chain of privations, exiles, and murders.

But the Mennonites were used to that. Originally of Dutch descent, those who settled in Russia had fled Holland to Prussia around the middle of the sixteenth century, seeking refuge from persecution. In spite of the fact that they made a great contribution to the agricultural development of Prussia, by 1786 their religious and economic liberty was jeopardized again. During the next century about half of them migrated to the steppes of South Russia, turning the undeveloped land into what later became the bread basket of Europe. The everyday language which they still spoke in modern times, *Plattdeutsch,* was a dialect which they had brought to Russia from the lowlands of Holland and Germany.

By their own hard work, their thrift, and their agricultural skills, the Mennonites had built a superior culture and had become, on the whole, prosperous. They had cultivated their land well, had built villages, and expanded industries, and had established good schools and large churches. Then persecution struck again, persecution because of their religious faith and also because of their economic prosperity. Private property was collectivized; once well-to-do farmers were arrested, imprisoned, and expelled to Siberia, never to be seen again.

Because the Mennonites had retained their German culture, many of them were evacuated beyond the Ural Mountains before the German Army entered the Ukraine during World War II. Religious privileges had been denied.

When the Germans moved into Russia for a short period of occupation, the Mennonites, along with all those of German background, considered the German Army their "liberator." Personal initiative was rewarded, religious life revived, churches reopened. Thus when in the fall of 1943 the Germans were pushed back, the Mennonites fled in their wake, some by train, many others by foot, still others on horseback and in horse-drawn wagons. Bitter hardships accompanied the journey as they retraced the steps of their forefathers; death was a constant companion.

Their lives were never secure. Always there had been grief and uncertainty. Always there would be. Maria could keep her faith—it helped her. But Hans had seen too much. If there was a God at all, He surely was a poor administrator.

"Hans, dear." It was Maria at his side. "Anni has decided to go on to bed. I think we should, too."

He choked back his anger and felt again that struggle within. Just as he would convince himself that all was evil and meaningless, as he would bow his neck in complete allegiance to infidelity, he would look down upon that face again. If there were no ultimate good, how then could Maria be explained? And how could the innocent

24

soul of a baby come from an abyss of evil? No one wanted to believe in futility; Hans pulled his living symbol of virtue close to his heart, glad to postpone the paradox of the coexistence of good and evil so long as she was near. Together they laid out the blanket on which Anni had been sitting.

No one slept soundly; Lenie whimpered often in her sleep, and the other children rolled restlessly around on their bed, tangling themselves miserably in their cover. Anni, partially relieved of her inner tension by talking to the Penners, slept uncomfortably, her head aching wildly in the morning as a result of her gruesome nightmares. When the sound of an early songbird outside the window announced the beginning of a new morning, everyone arose without being urged.

3

THE CHILDREN HAD GONE to school and returned again, marching gaily into the house to a new song they had learned. Hansie was, of course, hungry, but since the bread was scarcely sufficient for meals, he would have to wait. Rosie, eight years old and only two years younger than Hans, glanced around for a suitable place to take a nap, after giving an enlivened recitation of the day's adventures. School to the children was usually adventure, a happy change from the dullness of the room to which their father had been assigned in a greatly damaged part of the city.

Maria did not approve of everything the children learned at school, but she tried to give them Christian training at home. If she could only pass on to them a sturdy faith, their future would not be so perilous.

"Mamma, is Lenie well?" Hansie wanted to know, going over to his little sister and looking at her solicitously.

"No, Lenie is a little worse this evening, Hans."

"But last night when we said our prayers, we asked Jesus to heal Lenie."

"Yes," Rosie chimed in, "you read us stories about how Jesus heals people."

"We must keep on praying, children, but do you remember that we asked God to make Lenie well, if it is His will? When we asked Him to help us find Papa, He answered us with a 'yes,' but sometimes—" She stopped

26

to swallow a persistent lump in her throat. "Sometimes God knows better than people and has to make—different plans."

"I hope He makes the same plans this time," Rosie said, lying on the cot at Lenie's feet. Maria suggested that Rosie wash her face and hands, grimy from the day's activities. Though the children's clothes were patched to the nth degree, both children and clothes were amazingly clean, considering that Maria had no soap with which to work. Rosie's hair was always neatly braided, and Hans had brought the children long, white socks like the other children wore to school.

When evening came, Hansie studied as long as he could see by the light from the window. Rosie was fast asleep. Lenie had been whimpering, but lay quiet again, her face flushed.

"Her face is not a baby's face," Maria whispered, pushing a strand of hair from the forehead of her youngest. It was a tired little face, almost void of childish expectation. Born in November of 1944, soon after Hans had been drafted into the German Army, Lenie had been lugged around all of her two and a half years, taken hurriedly from place to place, ever westward. Tiny and undeveloped for her age, she had lived her short life without proper nutrition, with never enough milk, and always in an atmosphere of tension. Rosie, sleeping beside her, was a strange study in worldly wisdom, for she was old enough to reflect the fears of her elders. War, Maria thought, throws a cloak of maturity around her babies and marches her aged to their graves.

If only Hans, Big Hans, would hurry! Maria pulled the dark blanket over Rosie and stumbled toward the other side of the room, hoping that a glance from the window might catch him coming up the street. They would have to plead with a doctor to come, or else they would have to take Lenie somewhere to a doctor. Minutes dragged like hours as she lay there, tossing with fever. Maria repeated that Scripture over and over to herself, she tried to pray, she walked back and forth, she bathed Lenie's hot face. If she could only control the anxious beating of her heart! What time was it? She could go up and ask Frau Schmidt, but she didn't want to leave the children.

For what seemed the fiftieth time that day Maria tidied up the room, the crude furniture mute and cheerless. Over and over in her head drummed the words, "I wish he were here, I wish he were here—he must come—he must come."

As though her own motions would hurry Hans' arrival, Maria grabbed several potatoes from the sack, washed them, and put them in a pan to cook with the skins on. Then she walked swiftly over to the box where their tin plates were kept and, seizing them as though they were responsible for all her sorrows, placed them impatiently on the table. It was not like the mild Maria, but she was almost frantic to see the face of the man she loved. She listened for his quick step in the hall, but in vain. In vain she walked back and forth to the window, but his lanky figure did not appear.

"If Hans would only come! Ah, Rosie, my dear, you don't know how fortunate you children are that your father is with us again." She stopped by the cot to lay her hand on the soft cheek, then turned toward the window, afraid of the fear that was growing within her, her fear for the baby Lenie.

The jagged elbow bones of the bombed-out building across the street were almost beautiful, silhouetted against a pink patch of heaven that stretched across the horizon and fingered off into the green-blueness of the rest of the sky. Maria sighed, her starving soul drinking in the beauty in swift, glad gulps. Rosie stirred, reaching out her hand for Maria.

"Rosie, Rosie," she called softly, almost reverently, like the day she had shown the cathedral to the children. "Rosie, I want to show you something. Come here."

She gathered the still yawning child in her arms. "Know this one thing, my child. They can bomb the cities people build if they want to, but no one, no one has ever bombed one of God's sunsets."

And it was then that the door opened, and the two Hanses entered arm in arm.

Tante Friesen stood in the doorway, this time calmer than the evening before, but gravely concerned with the rest of the family about the baby. For Lenie lay fretting and complaining of pains in her head. Tante returned the affectionate hug which Rosie gave her, looking over her head at the serious parents who stood searching one another's eyes, silently consulting about what to do next.

"Why don't you, Hansie and Rosie, come over to my room for awhile? I'll tell you a story," she offered, seeing that the children did not comprehend the situation and were making a nuisance of themselves. She was not their real *Tante,* but among the German-speaking people any one respected because of age or position is certain to fall heir to the title of aunt or uncle. Though she had not the remotest idea of what the story would be about, she braved the ordeal and scurried the children through the door, closing it quietly behind her.

"Maria, dear, I talked today with one of my friends on the job about finding a doctor. That's why I was late. He told me that if I could scrape up the train fare to Kornrade—it's only thirty-five kilometers from here—he was sure the Evangelische sisters would not turn us away from their hospital. They are crowded—all hospitals are. But Lenie is so sick, they would surely make a place for her."

"But, Hans, you can't take a sick child like this on a crowded train. I almost faint when I'm feeling well and have to jam through the mob at the station. Perhaps in her weakened condition she would catch something even worse."

Hans leaned over to examine the tiny flushed face once more, then straightened himself to his full height.

"Certainly the other passengers on the train are human. They won't ask me to hang on the outside with the child, and one look at her will cause anyone on the train to give me consideration."

He was trying to be optimistic, but he was as worried as she, Maria thought, watching him from her seat on the edge of the cot. She saw him walk briskly over to the other side of the room, carrying the candle along with him to the corner where he had hidden the marks. She heard him whispering under his breath as he counted them, and she tried to shut out of her mind the song which the children were singing to Tante Anni across the partition.

"Are you really going then, Hans?" Her voice quivered

30

uncertainly as she asked it, for the thought of separation, even for a night, was a fearful one. So many of their Mennonite friends, thousands of them in fact, had been forcibly repatriated to Russia, that those still living in Communist-occupied territory were ever afraid of falling victim to the same fate.

"We had vowed that we wouldn't take another chance, even overnight. Couldn't we all go, Hans?" The question was ridiculously impossible and she knew it.

He had folded the marks in his own purse, had slipped them into his innermost pocket with his identification papers. Now he walked firmly over to her side and led her to the window.

"Maria, what else can we do but separate this once? We would barely have enough money to pay all of our train fare to the hospital, and then nothing would be left for the hospital bill or for food for tomorrow. If we did all go, where would we stay when we got there? The children will be so much better off in their beds here at home with you and Anni."

He paused.

"I know what you're thinking. Anni's nerves are on edge, and she has us all jumpy. But I don't think there's any reason to be afraid of—*them* for the short time I'll be gone."

In the light of the candle Maria was beautiful. Her straight black hair, knotted neatly on her neck, set off a sensitive face. It was probably her fine perceptivity of the feelings of others, as well as the suffering she herself had endured, that had caused her face to be marred with lines that had no business there.

Again Lenie gave a groan in her sleep, half opening her

eyes and asking for another drink of water. Maria obeyed with an eagerness that hurt, and Hans slipped his arms around the baby girl.

"Please take her and go, Hans. I—we'll be all right. Take good care of her and God will take care of us all."

Hans was suddenly practical.

"Is there enough bread here and a few potatoes to last until we get back? If the nurse gives permission, I may leave Lenie there and come back in time to go to work sometime tomorrow. I'll get full details to tell you, Dearest, and please don't worry. We'll come back as soon as we can."

He took her in his arms for one brief moment and whispered something in her ear.

"Yes, Hans, and you pray too, won't you? It does help."

He was not far from the kingdom. "I'll try," he grinned sheepishly as he lifted the child with tenderness, trying not to waken her. "Tell the children to come in, but quietly."

"Good-bye, Hansie and Rosie," he whispered a moment later, when they came hurrying in, laughing until they saw that something was wrong.

"Papa is going to take Lenie to a hospital. He'll be back soon," Maria explained, noting that Hans had leaned over and kissed them both. With many misgivings she kissed the warm forehead of their youngest once more and watched Hans stride confidently off, nodding lovingly to them, unable to wave because of the bundle in his arms.

She stood there in the doorway with the children for what seemed like five minutes before any of them said anything. Afterward, lying in bed, she wondered whether thoughts were communicated from mother to child. For it seemed as though her own troubled thoughts had rushed with the warm blood from her heart, down her aching arms, through her wet, clammy hands, through the finger tips that clutched Hansie's hand, and up to his young fearful heart.

"Mother," he had asked, keeping his voice under control only with great effort, "do you think Lenie will really get well?"

4

IT HAD BEEN A LONG, TEDIOUS DAY. Maria wondered, as she lay awake that evening between the two children, how she had ever endured it. Surely without God she could not have done so. All day she had been pacing to and from the window, hoping to see Hans and Lenie coming home to her again.

Unable to sleep, Maria had risen early and had knelt beside the window to pray. With so little appetite herself, she had increased the children's share of the morning bread. She had made the coffee-brew very hot, hoping that that would add to its doubtful nourishment. When it was time to go to school, she had prayed with the children, kissed them, reminded them not to talk about home or God to their friends, and had waved them off. She was scrubbing the floor vigorously when Anni came over before hurrying to the factory. Then everything was suddenly silent, much too silent.

Now Maria turned over on her hard floor-bed, careful not to wake up Rosie. Such a sweet child Rosie was, so genuinely helpful and so serious about everything. Hansie did tease her entirely too much, but on the whole the children got along well with one another. Maria had sent them both out to the park to look for wild flowers, for a few early violets could be found if they knew where to look. They had worked industriously, fixing up the room for Papa and Lenie.

It was too bad, Maria reflected, that her children had never known anything but the abnormal life of the trek westward. Always they were fleeing from the terror of Communist soldiers. Along with thousands of others like them, they had fled first to Poland, at that time occupied by the Germans. Surely, they thought, Nazism would be better than Communism. Maria remembered how grateful they were to have Hans along, because most of the women had already lost their husbands in Russia.

But all was not rosy in German-occupied territory. Hitlerism, which appeared to be the lesser of the two evils, was evil enough in itself. It was not long until the Germans, feeling that these delivered ones owed them a debt of gratitude, drafted their men into the German Army. Thus, what the Penners had dreaded for so long had come true. Maria and the children were separated from their husband and father, separated for a long time while Maria gave birth to their third child alone and fled with her little ones, ever westward. That they had been reunited after the war was a miracle, and Maria and the children would never tire of discussing the joy of it.

But were Anni's fears justified? Only tonight Anni, ashamed of adding to Maria's already crushing burden, had confided that a Mennonite family on the other side of town had disappeared in the night. Indeed, it was apparent that the Communists were determined to repatriate all of their wayward citizens. Anni still could not shake off the thought that she was continually under observation.

Maria would just have to get some sleep. She hadn't rested well the night before and had eaten little today.

35

What manner of woman would she be when Hans finally did come home? Determinedly she tossed about until she was a little more comfortable. Then she dozed, although she never was quite sure if she had really slept at all.

In her semi-sleep there had been voices: a woman travailing and crying with pain and fright, giving birth to a baby along the road. Maria, running with the two children, had seen her, but could not stop to help her because she was carrying a three-month-old baby herself. There had been the soft voice of the minister in Poland, that night when Maria found her peace. His was a soothing voice, telling the disquieted refugees that love, light, and hope could be found in a Person, in spite of wars and bombs and hate. Again, she had heard the voice of Big Hans, catching strangely as he looked at his family for the first time in more than a year. And then there was a voice, a raucous voice.

Maria sat up in bed. Until now she must have been dreaming. But this was no dream. She heard shouts right in the next room: Anni weeping, a deep voice giving orders, gruff angry words in Russian. She could not understand what the man said, but she knew what he meant. Stealthily she rose, rolled the children's clothes and her shoes in the blanket, and knelt beside Hansie.

The boy rolled over and opened his mouth to say something. Maria quickly clamped her hand over his lips. Shocked at her behavior and hearing the commotion next door, Hansie was immediately awake. Rosie, missing the warmth of her mother's body and sensing a disturbance, was also easy to waken. Maria whispered her orders sternly, stuck the bundle under her arm, and bounded out the side entrance, the children stumbling blindly behind her. They heard the steps creak beneath their feet, but they did not pause for breath until they felt the last step under them and smelled the freshness of the night.

Even then they did not stop. It seemed as though Maria's body was charged with incredible energy, as though her limbs were propelled by strength not her own. She took the children across the back lot, down by the gate, and over to the little side road that went out from the city in the direction of nowhere. It was a road they took when they wanted to be alone and talk together about nature, or about God, or about school. They did not look back; they said nothing. Instead they broke into a run, Maria almost carrying Rosie and holding her hand over the child's mouth to muffle her frightened sobs. Looking at Hansie, Maria marveled that he had had the presence of mind to grab his and Rosie's book bags.

"Mamma, let's go to the little spot where we have our picnics," Hansie suggested, his voice discreetly low. "No one would find us there."

She didn't answer him, but Hansie, even in his fear, was proud to see that when they came to the spot, Mamma took his advice.

They had not come here for a picnic since last fall. A picnic for the Penners was merely taking their black bread and any ration they were able to obtain and going outside to eat it. Somehow this added some taste to the skimpy meal.

Tonight, however, there was none of the usual splendor in the little spot. The low-hanging trees were almost bare, casting weird shadows against a cloudy night.

With the same dexterity of motion that had saved herself and her family, Maria laid out the blanket and told the children to sit down. Hansie sneezed and had no handkerchief. Quickly Maria handed them the clothes she had rolled in the blanket and put her own shoes on. Neither last night nor tonight had she undressed for bed, an almost uncanny intuition warning her that something might happen. As she sat there, praying, Maria felt another surge of strength; inward strength this time. She had to be the children's fortress; she did not dare let go to that nervous, dizzy feeling that came to her every time she thought of Anni Friesen.

"We will pray, children," she said, her arms around them both. "And then we will ask God where we should go from here."

The question had to come. It did.

"Mamma, where is Tante Anni going? Are they going to be mean to her? Will they try to kill her?"

The questions were from Hansie, but Rosie had stopped crying to listen.

Maria struggled with the words; they wanted to stick in her throat.

"Children, sometime God will punish all the people who do wrong in this life. We would have helped Tante Anni if we could have, but I knew that only prayer would help her. We had to go ourselves if we wanted to be safe."

Maria cried now, knowing that the release would do her good, then tried to think through her plans for the morning. With quiet words about the care of God she soothed the children into sleep on their cool, damp bed, waking them at the dawn of the new and unknown day.

5

MORNING SHUFFLED IN, dragging its feet and carrying the burden of the new day upon its back, its livid face expressionless. Maria met the day with equal lack of enthusiasm. Her head throbbed with unanswered questions; her heart beat out an anxious prayer. She sat for a few minutes, dreading the long walk ahead and looking at the two heavy sleepers curled up beside her.

Waking Hansie and Rosie was a herculean job, for the shell of unconsciousness which encompassed them was all but impregnable. When they did awaken it took them several minutes to be sure that the events of the night before were not a dream. But a look at their outdoor bedroom and the feel of the chill air convinced them of the reality of their new adventure.

"Mamma, where are we going now?"

"What happened to Tante Anni?"

"Will we find Papa and Lenie?"

"Mamma, I'm cold."

"Mamma, I'm surely thirsty."

"When and where will we eat breakfast? Will we have coffee?"

Maria tried to answer their questions patiently, wishing that she knew the answers herself. Yes, they would find Papa and Lenie first. No, there would be no coffee, but she had quickly salvaged the bread with their clothes the night before—they would have to be satisfied with the bread. No, they wouldn't go on a train; there wasn't money enough. They must walk many hours to the place where Papa had put Lenie in the hospital. Papa would see to it that everything worked out all right.

Fortunately it was a mild spring day. They passed without difficulty through the city that had for the past year been their home, and turned toward Kornrade by way of a dusty, narrow road. Signs of spring were everywhere; trees were just beginning to bud; little nameless flowers peeped out of clusters of grass along the road. Maria advised the children to save their breath and energy for the many miles they had to trudge, but their sudden bursts of delight when a rabbit crossed their path or a bluebird winged across the landscape comforted her more than she realized.

When Maria sensed that it was noon, they found a spot that pleased them and pretended their lunch was a picnic.

"I wish we had something to put on this bread. It gets so tiresome." It was unlike Hansie to complain about his food, so long as he had something to eat. Maria looked at him in surprise.

"We will accept God's gifts and be thankful, Hansie," she rebuked gently.

"If I were Frau Bornmann, I would be very thankful, because He gives her an awful lot," he commented, frowning studiously at his bread and scratching his head. "If God loves everybody alike, then why does she have that big house and all that food, while we have nothing?"

"Even Frau Bornmann has trouble getting food enough, Hansie. But you mustn't criticize God. What He doesn't give us in this world, He'll give us in the next. He loves us all the same."

Rosie had been listening intently. "That's an awful

long time to wait," she observed, eating her slice of bread slowly to make it last longer.

"When we find Papa, where will we go then? Will we go far away? Will there be a school there?" The subject again returned to the problems at hand.

Almost fiercely Maria drove away the despairing memory of a time, not too far in the past, when it was she who began and ended every thought with "When we find Papa," or "*If* we find Papa." If she had only followed her instinct that night when Hans stood beside her in the candlelight, gently fondling Lenie and making that momentous decision to go alone! They had broken their vow never to separate overnight, a fervent vow they had made that time Big Hans had been found. She looked at the Hans-in-miniature and noticed he needed a haircut badly.

"Well, we'll just have to wait and find out. The sooner we find him, the sooner we'll know." Maria rose, brushed the crumbs from her dress, and led the way back to the main thoroughfare.

The sun was high in the sky now; its rays penetrated their thin clothes and warmed their spirits.

Almost abreast of Maria's family another group of refugees also strolled along, packs fastened securely on their shoulders.

"Good morning." A girl of about eighteen with wind-rumpled hair and hardy complexion was gazing at the children, smiling as though the sight of them gave her new hope. "Are you going to Kornrade, too?"

"Yes, ma'am," Hansie replied. "I'm taking my mother and sister to Kornrade to find my papa and other sister."

The stranger tried hard to hide her amusement, then gave up and laughed outright. Two older women, bent

41

twiglike under heavy packs, grinned at Hansie appreciatively, as though for a moment he had relieved them of several pounds of the burden on their backs.

"I wish we had a boy to take care of us," one woman remarked, and Maria noticed that her face was an older duplicate of the young girl's, a little like Hansie was a carbon copy of her Hans. The woman's hair was fuzzy like the girl's, but streaked with gray.

"This is my mother and aunt," the girl confided. "We're heading west. Guess we'll have to cross the border 'black,' but we have high hopes. My name's Justina Schaeffer."

Maria felt Justina search her face for a return of confidence, felt her stare at her curiously. She had been almost tempted to walk ahead of this group, but the slow, even pace reminded her that on long trips no time was saved by hurrying.

"We're glad to know you, Justina. I don't know just where we're going except to Kornrade. Our baby's in the hospital there."

Maria bit her lip impulsively. After teaching the children to keep their personal histories to themselves, how could she so naively blurt out her destination to three complete strangers? But was there no one in the world whom you could trust? Something in the trio alongside her little family made her feel that here was friendship, genuine warmth beneath ragged coats and burdensome packs. Mutual need and common problems have a way of drawing people together.

"You have a baby besides these two?" The other mother cast her a sympathetic glance.

"Little Lenie is more than two years old, but we still consider her the 'baby.' She's little for her age."

"You just ought to see her," Rosie beamed. "She has black hair like Mamma's, but it curls up like Papa's yellow hair."

"My husband is with her at the hospital."

Maria reflected that she might as well finish the story, since the strangers were obviously interested out of kindness. They had been forced to leave their home during her husband's absence, she explained, and now they were joining him. During the brief rehearsal she eyed the children apprehensively, hoping that they would furnish no details. Talking of her hopes of reunion as established fact steadied her. The children walked confidently ahead, making little off-the-record remarks about the countryside, seemingly unconscious of the seriousness of the situation.

"It's still a little chilly for April, isn't it?" Maria noticed that Rosie's lips were blue.

"I'll be glad when the earth is really green again and the days warm up," Frau Schaeffer admitted. The wilted figure beside her nodded agreement. "We left Poland as soon as the weather seemed at all promising."

Justina swept her mother a troubled glance that frightened Maria, almost as though she were warning her to say no more. She had seemed so pleasant, but the muscles in her pretty face suddenly tightened. Maria didn't like the hard look she read there—she had seen it before. She glanced hurriedly at the face of the aunt, as one sweeps headlines in a newspaper, but there was nothing to be read on the expressionless mask.

"Hans and Rosie have attractive slate cleaners hanging from their book bags." Justina changed the subject quickly, eying the colorful knitted cloths which hung from the *Schul-Ranzen* strapped to the back of each child. Actually the book bags, now being used to carry the few groceries and extra clothing Maria had collected in those last frantic minutes, seemed a bit incongruous so decorated with the children's precious slate cleaners.

"We left in a great hurry, and had little time to collect ourselves," Maria apologized. "It was dark and I wasn't able to find my own straps, but the children's book bags were close and Hansie grabbed them." She sensed three pairs of eyes waiting for the rest of the story, but she didn't finish it.

"The children wanted pretty slate cleaners like their friends at school," Maria went on. "All the other mothers had knit such attractive ones, and children don't always understand why refugees must have so much less than others. So I sat down and reknit Rosie a sweater from a worn one I unraveled, using the rest of the wool to make their slate cloths."

"Children and war were never meant for companions." A brown hand slipped into a hidden pocket of Frau Schaeffer's coat, returning with a large, dark gray rag, wrinkled and much used. She wiped her eyes and gazed across the meadow to the little patch of forest in the distance. Maria noticed that Justina had, with forced disinterest in the older women's conversation, quickened her step to join the lively chatter of the children ahead. Hansie, aware that he was being observed from behind and perhaps even admired, had adopted a swagger which vibrated his slate cloth, knit in a solid color. His sister's, embroidered with a heart design, added a gay note to her old gray coat. The three bounced along several feet

44

ahead of their elders, substituting their own bright conversation for the sentimental talk behind them.

"We've heard plenty of rumors that things are better west." Frau Schaeffer stopped a minute to readjust the visible pack on her back; and the invisible one, the one filled with all the care and heartache of her existence, seemed to grow larger.

"If Justina can get good employment and for once can eat three square meals a day, maybe she'll be able to see something to live for. Sometimes, I tell you, I'm almost frantic to know what to do with the child. Before we started west—" She lowered her voice. "I tell you, she was as bitter as any young girl I have ever seen."

"Then having a goal—to be going somewhere—has helped to give her a temporary lift?" Maria had not lived the last ten years in vain.

"That's just exactly it. If we don't make it, if anything keeps us from crossing that border—" Her voice broke, but she felt with Maria there was no need to finish her sentence.

"I used to be that way, too, Frau Schaeffer," Maria said thoughtfully, aware once more of that peace down deep within herself. "It was when our home was broken up and my husband and I were separated through no fault of our own. I was really bitter. My spirits fluctuated with circumstances and the amount of food we were able to get. Then one day—"

She hesitated and considered whether she should tell it, but the intense gaze of the women beside her urged her on. She paused a moment to reword what she wanted to say. It was so hard to explain to someone who didn't understand.

"Then one day in a refugee camp in Poland something happened. Many people laugh at me when I tell it, but it is true, and without this experience I—I don't know what would have become of me."

Again Maria stopped for breath, realizing that the women were waiting curiously. She was also aware that Justina was listening and that her own two children were ten feet ahead, absorbed in some discussion of their own. She swallowed her pride and went on.

"My parents were Christians, and our family had always been religious. But for years we weren't allowed to have a Bible in our home. We weren't permitted to go to church. I had gotten so I thought of God in a far-off way, not as a real, close, loving friend.

"Our family has had a lot of trouble the last few years. I lost my parents. We lost our home and everything we owned. When my husband was taken, life seemed unbearable. The children and I and two of my sisters were herded into a refugee camp in Poland, along with hundreds of other refugees. You know what those camps are like."

Maria noticed that the women nodded their heads soberly. Only Justina posed indifference, as she swaggered her walk and froze the distant landscape with her cool eyes.

"There was a preacher in that camp, a Hugo Jung, who set up a chapel in a dilapidated room and preached night after night. He never seemed to get tired. Since we had nothing else to do, we carried our blankets and benches into that room and listened by the hour. He told us what we needed. There is a God of love, a Father who—who cares."

46

Her voice caught a little, but she continued. "The strange thing about it was that the camp was in a town called Kamenez, which means 'Stony City,' but it was there that my heart melted. Today I trust Christ, and I am no longer alone."

"Mother, did you see—" The children had slowed their pace to let the slower feet catch up. But Rosie knew when not to interrupt and, seeing her mother's face, she and Hansie blended into the background again.

There was silence, everyone snug in his own thoughts, behind the wall of his own reserve. Only Maria had let down the drawbridge to her private life. For a moment she was ashamed, wondering what had made her tell her most precious story, a pearl she had learned not to cast before swine. Actually, though, she had felt compelled to tell it. She felt her cheeks flush and her heart pound, not from walking, but from sharing her inmost life with those who might not understand.

"It must be wonderful to have faith," Frau Schaeffer finally remarked, after a silence that was heavy with emotion.

"It starts as a grain of mustard seed."

Justina's expression was no longer carefree as it had been when she walked ahead with the children.

"Oh?" She kicked a piece of gravel with her foot. Hard lines showed in her face as she spoke.

"Faith is for the blind, the gullible." Her expression softened as she saw her words sting the mellowed mother beside her. "I'm sorry, but how can you, how can anyone but a fool, believe there is a God in a world like ours? If you are not blind, then your God is."

They had been walking for several hours since lunch

and were beginning to see women along the road, old
women, middle-aged women, picking up sticks here and
there to carry back to their homes in the nearby city. As
though to illustrate Justina's acid remark, a little
withered old lady of probably seventy years, meagerly
dressed in threadbare clothes, appeared from the brush
at the side of the road to trudge heavily homeward. She
carried two bags on her back, one filled with tiny twigs
gathered along the way, the other with little chunks
of coal which she had no doubt picked up along the railroad. Although the sight of her proved that they could
not be far from their destination, although they began
seeing duplicates of her all along the way, her appearance
cast a shadow of greater gloom upon the small party.

"Ask that old Granny if she believes there's a God."

Maria did not answer. It was an old story. But the
fact that the words came from the mouth of a mere child
hurt her anew, made her pray that Rosie, young Hans,
and Lenie would be spared such a bitter attitude.

For a moment she saw again the multitude of people,
cattle, wagons, and autos rushing out of Stony City. She
heard again the shouts of impatience and fear and rage,
the wails of the old people, the cries of the babies. She
saw here and there a little child screaming for its mother
and a terrified mother reaching for little hands that had
been pushed from her own. She remembered that frightened crowd of people pushing ahead of the oncoming
army. She remembered how all of a sudden her sisters
were no longer beside her, how suddenly she had to
push on alone with the children. And then she had
looked to heaven and had prayed, and there had been
that wonderful closeness of her newly discovered Friend.

48

Others couldn't see Him; they laughed in her face; they screamed, "Where is your God?"

She did not answer Justina immediately. Walking took more strength than her scanty rations afforded; talking should have been eliminated except that she felt the words meant life to those to whom she spoke. Finally she answered, a little haltingly but with a new lilt in her voice.

"I know it sounds foolish to you, Justina, and it's not easy to explain. It's like a verse I read in the Bible once. Even though I may be cast down by the world, I am never forsaken by God. The Lord is my shepherd; I shall not want."

She did not say "Amen" but her soft voice had an "Amen" ring to it, and they walked on in the benediction of it.

It was with more humility that Justina finally spoke, noting with annoyance how interested her mother was in her reply.

"I'm sorry, Frau Penner, but I can't be that easily convinced. Your hypothetical God is a God of love. Yet—"

She hesitated and glanced experimentally at her mother.

"Yet outside my own mother and a few souls like her I have seen nothing in this world but hate. Oh, they preach love from the pulpits, but the preachers themselves would steal a load of potatoes if they had a chance. They deal in the black market like anyone else. I've seen 'God-loving' souls walk right out of church and pat their children on the back for stealing coal from a government truck. It's every man for himself in this world."

Seeing that there was little use in discussing the sub-

49

ject further, the group continued in silence, joined now by other homeward-bound pilgrims trudging beneath their sacks of potatoes, coal, or wood. For a number of miles Maria had noticed that it was the children, now, who could hardly keep up with the steady pace of the travelers. Turning around, she saw that Hans' heavy shoes were dragging and that there were tears in Rosie's eyes.

"I'm so tired, Mamma, my feet feel awful, and I think supper time will never get here. Can't we stop just once more? Just for a little rest, please?"

The women looked sympathetically at the children, but also glanced at the location of the sun, now spreading its bright wings across the western sky. Maria read their thoughts.

"We have made you stop so often, and it will be dark before we get to the city. We won't mind if you go on, though we were glad for your company." She knew that she would not have to walk alone, for now the cobble-stone street was heavy with traffic on foot, people hurrying home to their families after their days of scavenging, bargaining, or stealing a few things to keep themselves alive.

Justina was quick to take the cue. "I think we ought to go on, we can't afford to lose any time, can we, although it's been nice to talk with you."

A little reluctantly the older women agreed with the girl. They reached a tavern, dimly lighted, and Maria turned aside with her little ones, hoping to obtain a hot drink, at least for the children, at not too exorbitant a price. They said good-bye regretfully and parted, Maria wondering what, if any, lasting impression her words may have made. Hers was a simple faith. She knew of no complex answers to give to the complicated questions people threw at her.

They had almost reached the door when she was startled to hear a low voice behind her and to feel the sudden clasp of a hand on her arm.

"Frau Penner, thank you for what you said to us. Pray for us. Justina has been deeply hurt." Frau Schaeffer turned and hurried back to the highway to the others who impatiently waited for her there.

6

IT WAS MIDNIGHT. The part of the railroad station which had not been demolished by the blitz was cool as the night outside. Perhaps the dim lights made it seem a little warmer, but the floor beneath Hans' tired feet was possessed of a cold ugliness that crept up through his thin soles to the rheumatism in his legs. The atmosphere in the train station was dim with smoke. People huddled together on the floor to keep warm. Every now and then the cry of a baby went up from some large bundle of dark blankets, reminding Hans of his terrible errand. Today, after sitting at her bedside for many long hours, he had seen little Lenie pass away. How could he tell Maria?

Humanity was at its worst in a train station at night. Almost automatically Hans tightened his grip on the little worn purse in his pocket, passing swiftly by a group of hoodlums whispering together in a corner. But the hoodlums were not watching him; they were motioning toward a group of taffy-haired young women—girls who were out in the night making a living the sad, desperate way; girls driven to dire straits of immorality to earn a little bread for hungry families at home.

Had there been enough bread for Maria and the children while he was gone? Would the factory give him his job back after he had disappeared without any notice at all? What must Maria think by this time?

Diving out the west door of the station, Hans broke into a run, wondering if he should have wired Maria. He had told her before he left, though, that he would stay long enough for the child to have a thorough examination. And he couldn't wire her about Lenie's passing. He must take Maria in his arms when he told her; he must repeat some of her favorite Scriptures even though he took no stock in them himself; he must be there.

"Hey you, what's the hurry?" Hans felt his arm twinge with unexpected pain, as a green uniformed figure grabbed for him from the shadows along the sidewalk.

"Pretty late for a fellow to be in such a hurry. Probably not up to any good. Identification, please."

The policeman let go of his arm and watched him impatiently as he slipped his hand into that innermost pocket where he kept his identification card.

"My baby has just died in Kornrade. I am on my way home to tell my wife."

"A likely story." But the pleading eyes brought back to the other man too vividly a scene which he simply had to forget.

"Go on."

As the silent, black buildings began to appear in ghostlike formation in the moonlit evening, Hans' walk became a run again, a sudden surge of nervous energy making his tired feet light. The soft soles of his shoes produced the only noise that broke the awful stillness—awful, it was. Krauter, like any other German city, was a blacked-out vacuum at night. But tonight in his inmost soul Hans felt as though everything was too quiet, as though something was wrong.

Would he never get to Felderstrasse 21? He stopped

a moment and panted, then lengthened his stride once more, advancing upon Friedrichstrasse like a lion upon its victim. Frenzy, suspense, and nerves connived to keep him going, although he was running alongside the cobblestone road to keep from making undue noise. The moon had slipped under a cloud; the little side road was so dark that had he not known every step by heart, he would have slipped here into a ditch or there into a gully in the road itself. The foot bridge—he placed his hand on the railing to assure himself. The street sign—like a man reading Braille, he felt it warily. Then a left plunge, then the creaking wooden step under his feet.

"Maria!" He whispered the name, but he wanted to scream it. "Maria, Hansie, Rosie!"

"Maria, Hansie, Rosie!" Cautiously he felt his way over to the vestibule closet, feeling the floor to see if there might be a candle left. They had been so saving with those last few candles. Ah, here was one. Deftly he lighted it, stumbling uncertainly into their room.

His heart still pounding from his race with time, Hans leaned against the wall for support, surveying in the pale light the scattered possessions and the rumpled bed on the floor. It was not like Maria to leave the room so untidy, and a shudder crept up Hans' spine as he realized anew that something was very wrong. Frau Friesen's room, stripped of everything she owned, bare except for an overturned chair, puzzled him still more.

Hans buried his face in his hands, fighting despair, trying to think—think—think. Who might know where his family had gone? Why hadn't they left him a message? And then it came to him; if anyone would know, it would be Frau Schmidt in the attic. Hopefully his feet took the rotten steps three at a time.

Another set of rotten steps. Three soft knocks on an ugly door.

"Who in the world at this time of the night? What do you want?" A cracked voice came out through the hole in the door, angry, suspicious, frightened.

"Hans Penner." He knew it was Frau Schmidt.

"A moment, please." One latch removed, another latch, then an iron bolt.

"Hans Penner, come it. Sit down." She lighted a candle and the old mother slowly came to from her mat in the corner, taking in the scene at a glance, although her hearing was too poor to catch the conversation.

He could wait no longer. He was weeping and Frau Schmidt was obviously putting up a struggle to keep her composure.

"Where is my Maria? Tell me!"

"I do not know. Tuesday I left on my bicycle to bring back potatoes for the old mother. When I returned, the Penners and Frau Friesen were gone. My mother sensed a commotion, but she could not hear what was said. You can see nothing from this attic window. I ran to the neighbors and they told me that the Communists had come. They saw them take Frau Friesen, and since your family also disappeared at the same time—"

She could say no more. It was enough.

"Verschleppt!" It was as though a stick of dynamite had been planted in his soul for a long time and now suddenly had been ignited, an explosive blast that left him quaking like a house after a bombing raid.

Leaning with his back against the door, Hans no

longer wept. He stood with his fists clenched, his gray eyes wide, staring straight ahead, seeing nothing. His mouth was set, but his lip trembled. Thoughts too painful to entertain stormed into his tired brain, thoughts that had to be entertained, for they were facts.

A hand reached over and pushed a chair against his leg. Falling into the chair, he dropped his face into his hands—large, adequate hands that covered him from the compassionate gaze of the two women. Yet, he did not need that protection, for he knew neither where he was nor who was there. He knew only that Maria, Hansie, and Rosie were being loaded like cattle into some railroad car; that little Lenie was dead; that he was altogether alone.

"Please, a cup of coffee." Frau Schmidt had hastened to offer him the best that she had. He gazed at the kindly face, but he did not see it. How long had he been sitting here? His body had stopped trembling, his facial features were composed and expressionless, the ache was gone, his arms and legs were numb. Bitterness and defeat fell upon him like a dark garment. And now that hope had been murdered within him, his spirit also died.

"Please, please, a cup of coffee." This time he saw the tiny cup being extended toward him, took it without a word, drinking half of it.

"Take it away. She has none to drink. If I can't drink the cup which she drinks—"

His own words seemed to wake him from his trance. Across the room from him he saw the old grandmother Maria had told him about, propped up now on her pillows, weeping tears for his sorrow.

"But you are sure?" He addressed his question to Frau Schmidt, knowing the answer already.

"Who can be sure of anything?" Her voice softened. "Only of the love of the good Lord, can anyone be sure in these days."

"The love of the good Lord," he repeated, fondling the words. "Yes, Maria would have believed that."

He had to go, he heard himself say. But he wondered where, as he stood a little uncertainly, pushing the chair away from the entrance and grasping the broken knob of the door.

"Wait, please for one moment. There is something I wanted to give Maria. Perhaps it would be a comfort and sustainer for you."

The woman rose, stumbling over a pile of chips she had probably picked up along the street for kindling. Swiftly she removed a heavy tapestry from an old trunk and dived through a litter of papers, pictures, and linen. When she finally came up, she carried a tiny black book which she laid in his hands, her keen eyes watching his face for his reaction.

A Bible! How Maria had wanted a Bible! And now that she was gone—why had this woman waited? What would *he* do with a Bible?

"I can't accept it," he mumbled handing it back to her. "You must keep it for yourself."

Frau Schmidt wiped her eyes firmly, determined to control her emotions for the sake of this man.

"We have another Bible—saved both of them all during the war—kept them hidden. This is only a Testament. I was going—"

She stopped abruptly, trying to change what she had

started to say, but he sensed her hesitancy and his eyes insisted that she finish her sentence.

"I was going to give it to Maria for—her—birthday."

Her birthday! In all the anxiety of the last few days, he had forgotten that today was her birthday.

Slipping the Testament into the innermost pocket of his coat, alongside his identification, he opened the door. He paused for a moment to look at the two dim but tender faces, friends in his great need.

"Thank you. God bless you."

He replaced his worn hat on his head, pulled it down over his forehead, and turned to go. Then he turned back. He needed to have one more contact with a friend before he went out to face a friendless night.

"I am leaving this town and will probably never see you again. What you did for Maria meant a great deal to her. Pray for her."

But the woman, whose hand he had taken in a farewell clasp, was begging him to stay for one moment more.

"What do you plan to do now, Herr Penner? Do you know where you will go from here?" Her voice broke in her concern for him.

"I ought to go to Siberia and try to find them," he thought aloud. "Yet, it seems so useless—like suicide, almost."

He lifted his eyes, and his face was tired.

"I don't know. Good-bye. Thank you."

And he stumbled out into the night.

7

JUST ONE MORE VILLAGE, only a few more miles, and they
would be there. It was a pretty little town: old brick
houses hunched together, leaning on each other for support; ancient grandfather trees stretching out decrepit
arms, blessing the unassuming dwellings; occasional ill-
fed horses ambling along on the cobblestone street, bump-
ing wagons behind them with complete unconcern for
the riders perched high on their piles of junk or twigs.
It was a town that wore an evening sunset well.

Maria, her head throbbing, her bundle weighting her
down, trudged through the town with little notice of
the beauty of the lingering sunset. Her two little ones,
marching bravely on either side of her, said nothing, too
fatigued and heartsick to talk. Hansie made the remark
that his feet were so tired he didn't know where the road
ended and his feet began.

Maria looked with compassion on the two remaining
members of her family and promised that when they got
to the tall church in the center of town, now only a block
away, they would see if it were open. Maybe they could
rest on the benches for a few minutes and eat the last
fragments of their rations. There would be a treat: the
nurse at the hospital last night had slipped them a little
cheese from her own allotment.

Almost they had reached the door of the towering
church, all three of their souls reaching out for its protecting walls, their mouths watering for the beautiful yellow

cheese, when the sudden off-key clangs from the belfry of the church beat down like rain upon the village.

"What's wrong, Mother?"

"I'm sorry, Son, the suddenness and nearness of the bells startled me. Let's go in."

She turned to the right, noting that the door was open, and entered, sitting quickly on the first bench available. The children dropped beside her. Maria said nothing, but leaned the weight of her body on her arms, resting on the back of the bench in front of her while she listened to the lovely, resonant tones of the bells. Suddenly she raised her head to listen, realizing that the bells were spelling out a tune she loved.

"*Ein feste Burg ist unser Gott* [A mighty fortress is our God]," she repeated softly, and then whispered the rest of it to herself. How much those words meant to her! With trembling hands she broke the last small loaf of black bread into three pieces, two large ones and one small, and likewise broke up the cheese. Not that she cared if she ever ate again. But the children must, and she must too, to keep up her strength for what only the Lord knew lay ahead of her.

Ein feste Burg, ein feste Burg. Yes, God was her fortress and her strength, even now, but almost she had let Him slip, almost she had gotten like Justina, bitter and skeptical. She would never tell anyone, not even Hans, how frightful that moment had been last night when they had arrived in Kornrade and had been told that Lenie had passed away, that Hans had returned home that very evening. If the Sister had not been so gentle, so completely understanding; if she had not taken the children, fed them hot soup, and given them a bed, breaking the news to them, Maria did not know whether she could have made it.

"It was a case of advanced tuberculosis, rarely found in a child so young," the tall, grave nurse had told her, "and your husband stayed at her bedside until she died. By the time he got her here, her fever was treacherously high. The second day it was lower, but this afternoon it went up again, and the child passed quietly away." She cleared her throat awkwardly. "May God give you strength."

It was strange, ironical, how those rasping words had come back to her at the time, shot at her from a dozen cynical lips, "Where is your God?" She had been so sure, so very sure that Hans would be at the end of their day's journey, waiting to comfort her, to tell her that Lenie was going to get well.

She believed in the arms of God, she knew they were there, but they were not warm and material like Hans' arm about her. She was ashamed now of the way her faith had collapsed at the time she needed it most. Perhaps it was because she was so indescribably tired; she was not her real self.

"This is surely wonderful cheese, Mamma," Hansie said suddenly, his voice echoing in the empty church, his little-boyness once more coming to the surface with its cheer. 'Why aren't you eating, Mamma?"

"I was just thinking, praying a little, I guess."

She smiled down at him, a ghost of a smile really, but he took it as a live one. During the past day Rosie and Hansie had had little strength to go on, since their mother's courage, which they had relied on, was now crushed and broken.

61

"Church is where people usually pray, isn't it, Mother?" This from Rosie, also obviously to be making talk, to break this dead-weight silence.

She did not answer. The words she should have said lay heavy on her heart.

Hansie sat and studied for a long time, his bread and cheese gone, the church too dark to observe any such interesting things as its pulpit or the mice running to and fro among the benches.

"I don't think it's really much use to pray anywhere," he said philosophically, watching his mother out of the corner of his eye to see her reaction to this brazen statement.

Maria was still bent over, the one last bite in her hand yet untouched, and it was several minutes before she realized what Hansie had said.

"What? What did you say, Hansie?"

"I said I don't believe in praying anywhere any more, that's what I said."

"Hansie!"

"Well, we prayed that we would find Papa, and that Lenie would get better. We didn't find Papa, and Lenie —" It sounded awful to finish it; he couldn't bear it.

"Dear ones, we are going to go right on praying, the rest of our life. God hears our prayers and He is answering them, some way or other, but not always in a way we understand. As for Lenie, she is happier than she has ever been; she is not hungry; she isn't sick."

"You told us once the streets are made of gold, didn't you, Mom?" Hansie asked soberly, and Maria, looking into his inquisitive, dirt-streaked face, knew that he was no very stanch unbeliever.

62

"Yes, Son, it's more beautiful than I can tell you, and someday we'll be there together, enjoying it. We—oh, come on, children, we must go, or it will be dark before we get home."

Home? Could they go back to that building again? Would Hans still be close at hand? What would he think when he found her gone, and Tante Anni, poor Tante Anni! Frau Schmidt perhaps would let them sleep in a corner of her room. But if they found Hans right away, he would know what to do. The thought of being with him once more, of leaning on a stronger person for support and judgment, the very hope of it, gave Maria new vitality.

"Do you feel rested, Rosie?"

"Yes, but I'm awful glad we're almost there."

"So am I. If only there had been a train today, we wouldn't have had to walk back." Maria's heart failed her every time she thought of last night, how when she had finally come to her senses and had recovered from the shock of little Lenie, she had hurried down to the railroad station to inquire about trains. The dear Sister had offered them train fare. But she arrived only to see the last train pull out and to hear the news that there would be none on the following day because of the fuel shortage.

Maria helped Rosie fix her strap, brushed her hair back from her face, and checked Hansie's bag to be sure everything was in order. Almost ready to leave the large building, all three of them started, realizing that there was someone else in the room, entering from behind the pulpit. Rosie was frightened, and for a moment a weird little tune trembled on the strings of Maria's own taut nerves. Then she remembered.

"It's only the man who was playing the bells, children," she assured them. "Remember? *Ein feste Burg?*"

The musician appeared, a pinlike body, slightly stooped, topped with a steel-gray head. Still intoxicated with the charm of his own music, he closed the door behind him with care, walking slowly, thick brows knit in concentration, hands in pockets. Maria thought as she watched him that a man with a face like that would have to be either a very good or a very bad man, for his features were strong and definite, only a thin covering for intense emotions within. And the way he had played—

"Please don't let us startle you, Sir. We took a moment to rest when we saw the church was open." They stood in the little vestibule, ready once more to be on their way, yet eager for a look at the maker of the music that had refreshed them.

The old man surveyed his audience, taking in the usual ragged appearance and heavy loads of the refugees. Then his gaze rested on Maria's troubled face.

"We like your music very much, especially the message in the song you played."

"If it strengthened you for your journey, I'm richly repaid. Are you going far?" He paused a moment to take out the heavy keys from his pocket and closed the mammoth door.

The group of four turned together and walked northward, Maria explaining where they were going, somehow trusting this new acquaintance, and inquiring just how many kilometers they had yet ahead of them. She had long ago observed that men seemed always to know how far it was from any given place to another.

"Well, now, here's where I turn off. Let's see, I think you have about ten kilometers to the city. I trust you have a place to stay overnight? You look tired."

"Thank you for your kindness. Yes, we think—" Maria paused, remembering that around children one must be sure, "we're certain we have a place to stay. If we can only find my husband, we have nothing to worry about."

"And if you don't find him yet tonight?"

"We have a friend."

"Then may God bless you." And with that the old man shook hands with them in the same solemn manner that he had met them. Turning up a narrow, winding street, he disappeared over the hill, unaware that he was another living proof to Maria and the children that there was still goodness in the world.

"He was nice, wasn't he?" Rosie observed. "He reminded me a lot of old Grandfather."

"Grandfather couldn't play the church bells," Hansie argued, "and anyhow, he was even nicer than this man."

"Do you really remember Grandfather, children?" Maria asked in surprise. "You were very small when he passed on."

"I can just remember a little, how he had a beard, and how he would tell us stories. The rest I guess you told us," Hansie explained, for Grandfather had been so often spoken of that he was all but canonized in their minds.

"I remember how he died, too, along the way, and how everybody was so sad all the rest of the trek."

The evening shadows were deepening, and evening and death seemed so closely akin that Maria unconsciously hastened her footsteps and changed the subject, afraid that the children would once more talk of their beloved

Lenie. If they did not speak of her, Maria could go on, but sometimes today when they had discussed her passing, she had almost collapsed. Looking down at her charges, she saw Rosie nudge Hansie and whisper something to him.

"Don't talk about people dying. You'll make Mother cry." Her childish whisper came out loud and clear. Maria bit her lip and went on. Even losing five minutes might mean just missing Big Hans. If they found him, she could endure anything. If they didn't—

It was amazing how welcome a dreary pile of rubble, a street corner, a singular light, and a broken sidewalk could be, just because they were familiar. When Maria and the children finally hurried through the town, they thought they had never seen a city so beautiful as Krauter. Just outside the city they all sat down for a moment, Maria warning the children that there would be no more rest until they reached Frau Schmidt's.

She did not tell them how dangerous she felt it was to be walking side streets at night, how wary she was of sensuous soldiers, of strapping officers looming from behind a bush in the park or a doorway on the street. But she was afraid they could sense her insecurity.

Close to the train station in the center of town the streets were more heavily populated. Maria and the children wove in and out of the crowds; at times it was almost impossible to keep Rosie from being run down by a cart of potatoes someone had brought in from the country and dragged on and off the train. The closer to the station they came, the more activity and bustling could be seen, for everyone was anxious to get home, though home might be a hovel of despair. Maria caught Hansie looking piteously at a lad of his own age, standing off in the shadows, grabbing up cigarette stubs in his grimy fists as they were dropped by pedestrians. Everywhere faces were grave, bent on self-preservation.

Maria hated cities; she quickened her step and determined that when they got their family together they would head west once more, this time finding refuge in the country.

Left from the station, quickly past shadows, the endless blocks to Friedrichstrasse, then six more unlighted blocks. Maria paused before the front steps, unable to walk another step until she got her breath, her heart pounding blood into her face, her forehead, her ears. It was several moments before she noticed that Rosie was behaving strangely, suddenly throwing herself wildly against her mother and sobbing into her coat.

"Rosie, what's wrong? We're finally here. Why are you crying, Rosie?" Maria put her arms around the child and drew her to herself.

"I'm afraid, Mamma. *They—they* were in there—*they* —" Her voice broke out in a loud hiccoughy sob. *"They* took our Tante Anni. Papa isn't in there, I know he isn't!"

"But our dear friend Frau Schmidt is there, and we can stay with her. There are no—*they* aren't in there—not any more. I think, Rosie dear," she whispered, "that Frau Schmidt might have good news for us."

With that the three hurried up the steps, Maria pushing Rosie along with new strength, Hansie running on ahead, taking the steps two by two.

Had Frau Schmidt opened her door upon the pale faces of three ghosts, she could not have been more shocked than when she discovered the three tired, near-weeping figures framed in her doorway.

8

"AND THEN WHAT DID HE SAY? What did he say, Frau Schmidt, when you told him you thought we were *verschleppt?*"

"Maria, dear, he just sat with his face in his hands for what seemed to Grandma and me hours, I tell you. I never felt so sorry for anyone in my whole life."

"Did he believe you right away? Did he ask if there wasn't a chance you were mistaken?" Maria asked again. She had to know if Hans would be making any attempt to find them.

Frau Schmidt broke down and cried again in her already dripping handkerchief. "If I had only known—if I had only known! Why was I so sure you were gone? After all, it was only Anni Friesen that we knew to be *verschleppt.* The neighbor boy heard her voice crying in the wagon when they took her. And then you were gone, too. Oh, it's all my fault!"

Maria laid her hand on the shoulder of her friend. "Please, Frau Schmidt, don't blame yourself like that. You told him what you believed to be true. You can still help us if you'll only tell us everything you can remember."

Again the older woman tried to collect herself. "Well, I'll tell you everything I can recall. But you must spend the night here and we will make you as comfortable as we can while Grandma and I try to remember."

She spread out a ragged coat on the floor and made a bed for the sleeping Rosie.

"Here, Hansie, you lie down beside your sister."

"But I want to hear everything, too," Hansie objected. It angered him to be treated like a baby.

And so they went on into the night, Maria and Hansie cross-examining the two women, the women frowning in the dark as they tried to grasp every possible straw of memory that might help the Penner family. They described the rumors of Tante Anni's departure, the gossip that Maria and the children had been taken along, the despair of Hans, the gift they had given him, his parting words about trying to find them.

"Surely he won't do that, Frau Schmidt, surely he knows the futility of going into Siberia!" Anguish filled Maria's heart. "Oh, isn't this frightful! What if poor Hans would risk his life to find us in Siberia? I'm so confused I don't know where to turn."

"But he won't, I'm sure he won't. I wish I could remember just how he said it. Were you able to hear him, Grandma? He said, let me see, 'It would be suicide.' That's what he said, and I had the distinct feeling that he would not really do it."

Her words soothed Maria, and they all lay thinking. Frau Schmidt suddenly broke the pause.

"There was one thing I just can't quite understand that he said. Something about 'if I can't drink the cup that she drinks.' When I gave him a cup of coffee, that's what he said, and then he pushed it away from him."

Maria choked when she heard that, for in one warm moment Hans seemed very near, dear, loving Hans. Why, what he had said sounded like a scriptural quotation; it

70

was almost like what Christ had said in Gethsemane. Yet her Hans did not know Christ, the One who could make his burden lighter. Her pity for him, thinking that she and the children were suffering, was harder on her than her own dilemma.

Morning followed too closely on the heels of that disappointing night. Maria and the children slept a little longer than they ordinarily would have done, for they ached with fatigue and knew that there would be no guarantee of a bed in the evening.

"You feel you must be on your way—that you don't dare take another day of rest?" Frau Schmidt wanted to know, as she shared bread with the Penners that morning.

"I can see no point in waiting. Hans and I had always planned to go westward as soon as possible. We wanted to find a temporary home in the country where life would be more wholesome for the children."

She broke in three pieces the bread her friend had offered her.

"If I could only remember the route Hans had penciled on his map. One night we lay awake with a candle, making plans, trying to decide how soon we could afford to make the trip. Hans had a small map, but I do believe he has it in his billfold."

"Mamma." Hansie had been very silent and thoughtful, listening to her plans with sharp interest. "Mamma, I was listening that night. Papa was planning to go by way of Heuchlingen, I'm just sure."

Maria laughed in spite of herself. "You were supposed to be asleep. But are you sure, Hansie? Maybe we will find him if we take that route."

Rosie's eyes sparkled with hope. "We'll look for him

all the time we are walking, won't we?" she asked eagerly, and Maria was glad to see that she was once more herself after her night's rest.

Ursula Schmidt would never really forgive herself for misinforming Hans. Maria realized, with a twinge of pity for the good woman, that she would have given away her Bible and her last crust of bread if she could have in that way rectified her mistake. Indeed, she apologized so much that it almost wearied them and they were glad to get on their way once more, in spite of the fact that their destination was unknown.

"There are two things I must do before we leave the city, though," Maria said at length, "and the first thing is naturally to pick up the rest of our possessions downstairs. That is, if no one has stolen them."

Maria dreaded that ordeal, for she was afraid of the ghosts of memories that would haunt her, the chills that would run up and down her spine, when she looked into that room. She didn't dare remember—

And it was hard to keep herself from remembering. Not that she dared *forget,* but it hurt to recall—baby hands outstretched toward her—first words—a bewitching little face—warm, strong arms about her—the peaceful security of her husband's presence. All these things she took for granted when they were hers, but the memory of them ripped the very seams of her heart when they were gone. How much easier it would have been to carry the wiggling form of Lenie than it was to bear the burden of grief that was hers, to feel the terrible emptiness of arms that should have held the child. Yet, thoughts of Hans were hardest, for Lenie was safe and happy with God, while anything could be happening to Hans.

72

"And what is the other thing you have to do?" Frau Schmidt broke in on her thoughts.

"There is only one possible clue to finding Hans. We must go check at the factory to see if he stopped to get his pay. Of course, he must have. He needed it."

"Aren't you afraid of having to make explanations, of perhaps bringing suspicion on yourself and the children?"

Maria finished braiding Rosie's hair and gave her own a final twist.

"Frankly, I am, and that is why I am not going to the ration office to notify them I am leaving. But we'll have to take a chance at the factory. Hans has a head start on us, to be sure, but we must do everything we can to find him."

It was not a very attractive part of town. Maria hustled the children past ugly buildings, past undernourished children who played and found mischief in the streets, past smoke-covered men who silhouetted the thin morning sunlight.

"Mom, what's that whistle for?" Hansie wanted to know, as they hurried through the door they thought was the right one.

"I don't know." Maria hadn't even heard a whistle. Children could be so irrelevant sometimes.

"Hans Penner?" The man they finally found who should know, after timid inquiry of at least a half-dozen workers, seemed no more interested in their problem than the cold-shouldered building they had entered.

Sitting down at a cluttered desk and opening his payroll book, he glanced nonchalantly through the "P's." "Oh, yes, Hans Penner. He's the fellow who came in yesterday morning—didn't have too much coming to him —was crazy to give up a good job."

Maria almost jumped. "Then—then he did leave! Where did he go?"

The man stared at her incredulously. "How do I know where he went? Do you think he told me his life history?"

Risking his ill humor, Maria pressed the point.

"Would anyone know? He's my husband. I must find him."

There were tears in her voice, but it did not help. Slapping the pages of his book together, the man lighted a cigarette.

"He went out that door, and I suggest you do the same." He swore a little and then growled under his breath, "These———refugees are surely a nuisance."

"Well, now what?" Hansie's lower lip trembled as he looked at the pained face of his mother. He stood on the sidewalk with his hands on his hips, his eyes focused angrily on the door.

"Wasn't he mean, Mother?" Rosie asked softly. "Why, he almost made me cry."

He did make me cry, Maria thought. *But I am going to have to be strong for the children and keep my tears on the inside.*

"I just hope something terrible happens to that man sometime," Hansie sulked. "Something awful, like—"

"Hans!"

"I didn't really mean it," the boy backed up. "But he was so hateful. I wonder how he'd feel if—"

Maria took her son by the shoulders and gave Rosie a gentle push.

"We must be going, children," she said sternly, bracing

74

herself for another long day of walking. "We'll head for Heuchlingen and see how far we can get along. But keep your eyes open for Papa. He may not have left Krauter yet."

"But where will we sleep tonight, Mom, if we don't find him?"

"God will find us a bed somewhere—" Her voice trailed off in uncertainty. And then she realized again what a poor hypocrite she was before her children. Looking down at her thin, peaked offspring she saw the same fears, the same perplexity, the same grief that wanted to trouble her, mirrored in their young faces. It was not right that it should be so.

I must have more faith in God, she thought to herself, as they made their way once more out of Krauter, once more feeling the ground beneath them through their paperlike shoe soles, once more homeless nomads tramping toward an unknown future. *I must trust in God— I must—I must—I must.*

9

"IT'S GETTING DARK, MAMMA."

She knew it. Hansie didn't have to remind her that it was late. Her head reminded her, the way it thumped. Her feet reminded her, the way they ached. Her back reminded her, the way it groaned beneath its load. Her nerves reminded her, the way they made her want to snap at the children.

Why hadn't she tried to find a place to stay in the last town? She didn't exactly know, only that a sudden, uncanny fear had gripped her and her nerves had shoved her onward. Maybe it was God speaking to her. Maybe it was only her nerves. She didn't know. She was almost too tired to care.

For now Maria was not so particular. She would take anything. Anything that furnished a roof over their heads and a little protection from the early spring air that chilled their bodies and spirits. It would not matter if it were dirty—they couldn't get much dirtier. It would not matter if the bed was hard; when you got this tired, you could almost sleep standing up. She was even too weary to have nightmares.

The thing that grieved her soul the most was that Hans, quite alive and strong of muscle and sinew, was also drifting about, perhaps not too far away, needing her as much as she needed him. All because of a series of fantastic mistakes. Why, why did it always have to be like this? O God, would they never know normal family

76

life again? Would they always be losing one another, fleeing from terror, living like tramps along the road?

But no sooner would Maria give way to these thoughts than she would look at the tender faces of her children and, with tears running down her cheeks, she would repent of her rebellion.

"O Lord, forgive," she would pray and, simply trusting that He had forgiven her, she would press on.

Suddenly she stopped short in the road, and, taking Rosie's hand in hers, squeezed it warmly.

"Children!" she exclaimed, and the children saw what she had seen ahead, rejoicing at the old familiar tone of hope in their mother's voice. "Children, ahead is a German *Gut*. Maybe somebody there will take us in for the night."

Automatically stepping up their pace, they were not long in arriving at the village, surrounded on every side by the many acres of fields that the villagers farmed for the owner of the large estate.

"Rosie, what are you crying about?" Maria looked in surprise at her daughter, one moment before as brave and hopeful as her brother.

She shook Rosie vigorously. There just was no time for tears.

"Rosie! What is the matter?" She felt irked and impatient. If they wanted to go to bed, why didn't they co-operate? The tears streamed down her face as she realized that they were only children and that her weariness was almost overcoming her.

"Mamma, I'm afraid they'll say 'no,'" Rosie exploded. "Then what in the world would we do, Mother, what would we do?"

Her answer soothed the child. "They won't refuse us, Rosie, I know they won't."

It would never do, Maria thought, to let Rosie sense her own misgivings. Even though it would be a pretty hardhearted person who would refuse lodging to a mother and her children on such a chilly, damp night, there was something else that bothered her.

For Maria had heard a great deal about these *Guts,* large estates farmed by peasants who lived together in little central villages. Before the war the peasants were treated well. They lived contentedly in their small houses, worked for the owner of the estate, kept their own pig and chickens, and sent their children to the nearby school. Relationships with the owner, who always lived in a large house close by, were usually good. He owned the cow, but they got the milk. He owned the farm, but they had enough to eat. And their homes were furnished comfortably.

When the Communists would take over a village, however, the owner's properties were not only taken away from him; he was either *verschleppt* or he was permitted to move into one of his tenant houses and work like the other villagers. The soldiers, who lived in the large homes on these estates, were not too bothered about the villagers, but Maria did not feel comfortable at the thought of being that near the Communists for very long.

"Pardon me. What is troubling the little girl?"

Maria jumped. She had not noticed the dark, bent, old figure of a woman who stood looking down at Rosie.

"We are looking for a place to spend the night; just any place will do—a shed or a barn or a cellar or an attic." Maria had spent many a night in everything from a damp

78

bunker to a pigpen, and she knew that refugees could not afford to be particular. She hated to beg! But tonight she knew that she must.

"Please," she cried, "if we can spend the night in your quarters, we will be willing to sit in any corner. Please don't send us away."

The old lady looked again at the weeping Rosie, then glanced nervously up and down the street.

"Then come, come quickly," she whispered. "Father and I will put you up."

Entering one side of a two-family house, they stumbled into a warm kitchen. For a few dizzy moments Maria saw only through a blur of tears, but before she could clear her vision, she was ushered into a chair by wrinkled hands. And as she wiped her eyes to look around, she saw that the children's backs had been unloaded of their bundles and that they, too, were seated on stools close to the wood stove at the west end of the kitchen.

"You are hungry and Father and I were just about to eat our evening meal. Do you have any rations with you?"

Maria shook her head, unable to speak. They had eaten the last of Frau Schmidt's bread at noon. She had wanted to save some but it was obvious that the children needed it. So she had had to depend on the Lord beyond the noon meal.

"Then we will share with you," the low, shaky voice assured them. "We are having potatoes and clabbered milk for supper. I will add a few extra potatoes tonight, and we will have a special treat. We'll have coffee."

"But—but we hate to eat your rations," Maria objected weakly. "We will never be able to pay you back."

79

"It doesn't matter. You aren't the first family we have lodged for the night. Perhaps I will fry the potatoes tonight instead of cooking them in their skins. They will get done a little sooner. Take off your coat, please—why, we don't even know your name yet."

"Penner—Maria, Hansie, and Rosie. Please tell us your name, too, Grandma. You are so kind. You—you don't know what this means to us."

"I think I do. My name is Erna Maier and my husband is Wilhelm Maier. He is upstairs looking at our supply of wood. He will be surprised."

Maria took off her shoes, moved closer to the fire, and sank farther into her chair. "Then we will call you Grandma Maier, if that's all right."

Her eyes followed the new friend around as Grandma tried to hustle her old body to get their meal. The children watched too, with interest. Grandma Maier was supple for her age. She was dressed in a dark, long-sleeved dress and a large, print apron, patched colorfully.

"Mamma, I'm afraid I'll have to replenish the wood supply. I don't believe it's going to last." They had been hearing heavy footsteps in the room above the kitchen, and now a tottering old man appeared in the stair door beside the stove. Rosie, not yet at ease, gave a startled little cry.

Grandma Maier's face crinkled into a smile.

"It is only Father, child. Father!" She lifted her voice and her words came forth with new resonance. Apparently the old man was somewhat deaf.

He glanced in surprise around the kitchen and then looked questioningly at his wife, who begged him with her eyes to understand.

"They had no place to spend the night and no food, Father," she explained, and the knife in her hand trembled. "Is it all right?"

He stroked his beard and looked thoughtful, first at one and then the other. Finally, his eyes rested on young Hans and filled with tears.

Forgetting to acknowledge the introductions which his wife had hurriedly made, Father searched Grandma Maier's face.

"Did you notice?"

"Yes, I did. And the girl, too."

He looked at Rosie for a long moment. "Yes-sssss," he finally agreed. Remembering his manners, he shook hands solemnly with each member of the family.

"Of course they may stay, Mamma," he replied benevolently. "Have I ever been one to send a child out into the night?"

When supper was almost ready, Grandma poured some hot water from a dilapidated teakettle into a washbasin.

"You will all want to wash now, and perhaps bathe sometime before you leave again in the morning." She hesitated. "Or whenever you decide to leave; there is no hurry."

And then they ate, Grandfather helping the children to their food, and Grandma obviously enjoying her bustling for the sake of these new friends.

Maria did not know whether the old couple would have bowed their heads in thanksgiving or not, had she not instantaneously done so. Limping along from one meal to the next, Maria knew how to be thankful. It was a lesson she could never forget.

10

IT WAS MORNING, late morning. Maria had no idea what time it was, but she did know that she had not felt so rested in weeks. She stretched and yawned and gazed affectionately into Rosie's sleeping face Then she hurriedly dressed and went into the kitchen.

Hansie was up, investigating everything about the house and asking questions. Breakfast, which consisted of potato soup, gave off a tempting smell. Grandma Maier turned spryly, smoothed imaginary wrinkles from her apron, and smiled a "Good morning." Grandpa, grinning through his beard, looked up briefly from a chat with Hansie. Suddenly Maria felt that she was at home, in a real home with warmth and love and cheer. Laying the plates on the table, heirlooms which Grandma had taken from her living room cupboard for the occasion, Maria could not help thinking what her children had missed in life.

When breakfast was over, Grandpa Maier looked significantly at Grandma and suggested that instead of washing the dishes, they all go into the living room and become acquainted. He felt that he could not stay away from his work very long and that he would not want these guests to leave until they had learned to know one another better. Rosie by this time had joined the group and they sat around in the little living room, visiting in the pleasant, easygoing way that old people love.

"You were very tired last night, weren't you?" Grandma Maier began. "How far did you come?"

And then Maria told her story, starting with her separation from Hans and Lenie's death, and occasionally referring to times previous to that. She felt none of her usual restraint. These people were friends.

"But I have only talked about us," Maria finally said. "Do you folks have children?"

The old couple became silent, and Maria wondered if she should have asked. Then, very deliberately, Grandpa answered, bringing forth his reply with the same respectful, cautious care with which they had brought their best china from the cupboard.

"We had two children, just as you do here, and they differed in age about the same as Hansie and Rosie." He paused to pat Hans on the head, which gesture Maria knew was not too much appreciated by her son.

"But Martha and Peter did not stay little. Peter was killed in the *Wehrmacht* and lies in a field in France. Martha—"

He was careful that his eyes did not meet his wife's.

"Martha just would not stay at home as we wanted her to. When she was twenty-one she went to the city (Berlin) and got herself a job as maid. There she met a likable chap and they married. They had three sweet children, just babies."

He stopped for a long time to regain his voice. Then, unexpectedly, Grandma filled in the rest.

"During the American air raids, their house crumbled into many pieces. Of course, they all died. Our cousin wrote us of it. We did not even get to have a funeral. Cousin went to the heap of rubble which had been their house and put up a white cross and said a prayer. It was all the funeral they had."

"I guess you know what Berlin looks like since the war," Grandpa asked, trying to shift the topic a little from its most painful point of focus.

"We lived in Krauter, you know," Maria responded. "It got blasted pretty badly. But from all we have heard, Berlin must be much worse."

Grandpa dropped his head, as though he carried all the shame and folly of his generation upon his own shoulders.

"War," he gasped. "How foolish it is! Oh, may there never be another war!"

He stayed submerged in his own melancholy for several moments, then lifted his eyes and looked at Maria.

"Where are you going now, my dear?" he asked earnestly.

"I don't know," Maria replied, wishing that he would not bring up that subject so soon.

"You see," she continued, "I have no idea whether there is any use trying to find Hans. And then, too, we have to stop somewhere and get some rations or we will starve along the way. Eventually we want to try to cross into the western zone."

She lowered her voice. "Because that is where we know Hans is headed for, and that is where we will find him."

Grandma's eyes filled. "You are brave, maybe too brave."

"God will take care of us."

Again Grandpa cleared his throat and looked almost beseechingly at Maria.

"You know," he said, glancing first at Hansie and then at Rosie, "you know, Frau Penner, your children remind Grandma and me a lot of our own two when they were young. Last night, after we went to bed, we talked a long time. We are very old people, and we can hardly care for our four acres of land, to spade, to plant, to cultivate, to harvest, to gather wood, to milk the cow, to care for the pig and chickens. We can do some of it, but I'm getting to be a tired old man. I've lived my day, and done my work. But Grandma and I must keep on working. We must keep on appearing to get things done, or I'm afraid we, too, will be out of a home."

He spoke slowly, frowning and thinking hard as he went along.

"And so last night, Mamma said to me, 'Father, we've got enough room for the Penners. We're lonely, and they seem to be good people. Maybe if we pooled our energies, we could all live off this farm. Let's invite them to stay.' "

Maria looked from one to the other of the old people, and her heart beat violently.

"How good God is!" she said at length, swallowing hard. "How good God is!"

And then a cloud passed over her soul. She dared not sacrifice her ultimate purpose of finding Hans for the sake of their temporary comfort.

"But Hans, my husband! I cannot believe that he was foolish enough to look for us in Siberia. And if he did not, who knows but that he might be close at hand. How can we know?"

Grandpa frowned again, stroking his beard as though by that mannerism he could think more clearly.

"He has a head start of one day over you?"

"Yes, he has a start of two nights and a day over us. Of course, he would have had to rest sometime, too."

"How do you know he is taking this route?"

"We don't. Once we had planned to come this way."

"And he is a man," Grandpa continued, "and a man can travel much faster than a woman with children."

"I know that well."

"And you have no proof that he did not head for Siberia?"

Maria trembled and shook her head.

"If you leave today or tomorrow, you still have no food, very little clothing, and no shelter above your heads."

He had been doing her thinking for her. Maria dropped her eyes and stared unseeing at her folded hands.

"O God," she prayed, "tell me what I ought to do!"

And when Grandpa spoke again, it seemed as though God spoke through him.

"Why don't you stay and get your ration business straightened out, get your health built up a little, and write to the Red Cross in Berlin to trace your husband's whereabouts? Surely he will report when he gets another address."

"But he thinks we are *verschleppt*. He might not bother to report."

"Have you no other relatives he might be trying to locate?"

Maria shrugged her shoulders. "We don't know how many are even living. It's doubtful if any of them are this far west. Most of them we know to be in Siberia."

"Still, if he is wise, he will register in Berlin."

"But if I would stay here, what of the Communists? Are they not in charge of this *Gut*? I've told you where we're from. We're in constant terror of repatriation."

"Of course, I understand. But we are not treated cruelly by the Communists, so long as we do our work. They don't bother us nor pry into our affairs. They seem to be too interested in their own business to care much about the villagers. And we villagers stick together. Nobody will tell anything on anybody else in this *Gut*. I don't think you have anything to worry about."

His voice was confident, and Maria's cloud vanished.

"Then—then we'll stay, won't we, children? We'll stay until God sends us forward again, stay till we have helped you both as much as we can and till we are again strong enough to go westward. Yes," and she smiled as the children gave a shriek of delight. "Yes, we'll be very glad to stay!"

11

"DON'T YOU WISH vacation would last forever, Friedrich?"
Hansie asked his friend as they ambled slowly home from
school one warm day in early September. He thought
nostalgically back to that short month of July. Then
school was not in session; he and Grandpa Maier could
work side by side all day long; he and Friedrich could
play after their chores were done without having studies
to shorten their carefree hours. What fun they had had,
whittling with an old knife of Grandma's, chasing one
another around the house, teasing their sisters, bending
over like hairpins in laughter at their own good jokes!
And then before bedtime Grandpa could always be
counted upon for a story, sometimes exciting, sometimes
a little dull, but a story nevertheless.

"Oh, I don't know," the studious Friedrich replied,
"I get awfully tired of all the work we have to do during
vacation month. I'd rather be going to school. I like
school."

"You would!" That was one point where Hansie and
Friedrich could not see eye to eye. But Hansie knew
there was no use pursuing the matter further.

"I certainly wish we could find another rabbit," he
said, changing the subject amiably. There was always
good response when the rabbit story was mentioned. It
was the most amazing thing that had ever happened to the
boys, wonderful because of the joy it brought their parents, wonderful because of the way it had smelled when

Grandma had fried it and the way it had tasted when their families sat around devouring it together.

"And you know, Friedrich," Hansie boasted, "if I hadn't had the nerve to follow those hunters, we wouldn't have gotten the rabbit. You were afraid."

"I was *not* afraid. I was just being sensible. We were just lucky, that's all, that they didn't see us. And they didn't see the rabbit."

"We were lucky, too, that we didn't know who the hunters were or where they came from. If we had, Mom would have made us return the rabbit. Because it really wasn't ours."

"But we didn't know," Friedrich said triumphantly. "My mother said it was manna from heaven, or something like that."

No, they would never forget the rabbit. They had been walking home from school soon after Hansie had come, learning to know one another fast, talking about so many things, when they had heard shots. Hearing brisk male voices only a few hundred feet away, they had hidden in the tall grass. Then, as soon as the hunters had gone on, they had sneaked over to where they had heard the shots and looked around. Suddenly Friedrich stumbled over a warm, moist something in the grass. It had been a dying rabbit, shot but undetected by the men.

What rejoicing! Friedrich's folks, who lived in the other half of the two-family house the Maiers occupied, had come over and helped in the preparation and had added a few of their own potatoes to make the meal complete. Mamma Penner had asked the blessing and while everyone looked on with mouths watering, the rabbit had first been passed to the two young heroes for their choice of pieces. There had been no meat in the house before or since. Truly that was a day worth telling their great-grandchildren about!

"Yes," Hansie said as though to himself, after they had stopped to rest and make themselves toothpicks out of sharp twigs, " I surely do wish we could find ourselves another rabbit. Grandpa promised we would try to make a trap this winter. He said maybe the Commander might even give him permission to butcher his pig this winter, though he hates to ask it because he might never get another one. But now the vegetables in the garden are all gone and our potatoes are pretty scarce. Grandpa is getting a little worried."

Hansie frowned as he thought of someone else who was getting anxious, his own mother. It hurt inside when he thought of her, always tired, sometimes a little sick, lying down because of dizzy spells. And it hurt even worse when he thought of what she had said to Grandma and Grandpa Maier only last night. No, no, that dared not happen. They dared not leave the Maiers, not now. But Mamma had said they might have to do that if they were eating up food which Grandma and Grandpa needed themselves. And if they had to leave, they had better go while the weather was still warm enough to walk.

During the summer the food had easily reached. There had been apples, lettuce from the garden, enough milk to get along, and potatoes, in addition to the one loaf of heavy black bread which each person got per week. There had been sugar-beet syrup for the bread, too. Potato soup without milk, or potato cakes, usually made up their breakfast. Lunch consisted of a thin milk soup with little flour patties floating in it, or, occasionally, fried potatoes with barley coffee poured over them. For supper they ate potatoes cooked with their jackets on and clabbered milk.

Grandpa and Hansie had enjoyed gathering wild berries in July, after their day's work in the fields, for the fresh wild fruit had made a sumptuous change in their diet. But now that the summer goodies were gone, the family menu was again essentially a limited supply of milk, potatoes, and black bread.

"Friedrich," Hansie blurted out, and it went hard for him to ask it, "Friedrich, what would you do if I should leave?"

The heavy book bag almost fell from Friedrich's thin hand. "What do you mean, Hansie? You aren't leaving."

"We might."

"Why? Why do you have to leave?"

"Mamma figured up the potatoes that came out of our garden this year, and there are just enough to keep the old people all winter. There aren't enough for all of us. Without potatoes we will starve. You know that."

"But what would Grandpa Maier do without you?"

Hansie thought it over for a moment, and it gave him an important feeling to realize the truth of what Friedrich had said; a wonderful, satisfying feeling that he was needed. Maybe that is why he had never minded chores as Friedrich did, because he knew that the way he helped Grandpa Maier made him an essential member of the family.

After all, who carried the water from the village pump in the evening? Who helped Grandpa cut the winter's supply of wood? Who carried all the wood upstairs and stored it neatly in the attic? Who supervised Rosie when they went out gleaning extra wheat to take to the mill? Who pitched right in like a man and helped bind wheat behind the cutting machine? Who would soon begin to dig sugar beets at almost the rate of a man? Who helped Grandpa every evening of his life? Hansie! And Grandpa was not short on his praise of the boy.

"I know Grandpa would have an awfully hard time getting along without me," Hansie admitted, trying to look modest as he said it. "I don't see how he ever managed before I came."

"I still don't think you have to go!" Friedrich puckered up his brow as he did when he was trying to work out a difficult problem in mathematics.

By this time they were nearing the large villa that had once housed the owner of the *Gut*. Although they usually looked hard when they passed, to get a glimpse of what might be going on in the "Great Unknown," Hansie and Friedrich quickened their step.

"What makes me so disgusted, Hansie," Friedrich muttered under his breath, when they had passed the villa, "is that you might have to leave because there isn't enough food, and those officers are going to waste a whole field of carrots again this fall like they did last year."

"You mean they aren't going to do anything with that big pile of carrots over there?"

"Last year they didn't. Just let them rot. And all of us so hungry for them we could hardly stand it. But everyone was afraid to do anything about it."

"I wouldn't be afraid."

"You would, too!"

"No, I wouldn't, Friedrich. Remember the rabbit. You were the one who was afraid."

Friedrich flushed with anger. He got tired of Hansie rubbing that in.

"All right, if you're not afraid, why don't you go over and get some of them right now—take them home, smarty!"

"How stupid do you think I am, to try it in the daytime? I'm serious, Friedrich. After dark, who would see us?"

"They would!"

"No, they wouldn't."

He stopped and looked back, now that they had gone around the bend in the road and were out of range of the large house.

"Look, Friedrich. After the chores are done, when it's almost dark, too dark to be seen easily and yet light enough to see where we are going, we could slip away from the house and go over through Fetzer's back field and sneak a few of those carrots home."

"That would be stealing."

"No, it wouldn't, not if they aren't going to use them anyhow."

"I—I guess that's right, but what if we got caught? Our folks might never see us again, not to mention the carrots."

"Don't be silly. They aren't watching that carrot field at suppertime. They're either eating or drinking. Remember that time—?"

Of course, Hansie knew that Friedrich remembered that time a few drunken soldiers had given them all such a scare by banging on their door in the middle of the night. The soldiers could have been penalized for it had they ever been found out.

"Well, you can do it if you want to, Hans, but not me. I like being alive too well."

"You're always a coward. I shall leave remembering you a coward."

Hansie was sure that this technique would get results. More than once he had used the rabbit incident to his own advantage in pressing his friend into adventure.

"All right," Friedrich finally agreed. "But remember, it was your idea, if anything happens."

"Yes, and it was also my idea when our families sit around the table for a carrot feast," Hansie grinned.

"What time shall we meet?"

"I'll come to your place and ask if you can play."

"My mother will say 'no,' if she finds out how much studying we have to do tonight."

"I'll say it is just for a little while, that I want to show you something. Agreed?"

Friedrich hesitated and frowned.

"Agreed."

12

It was dusk, that indefinite time of the evening that was neither night nor day, the blue-tinted hour when Mamma tried to remember verses she had read in Frau Schmidt's Bible. Supper was over, and Hansie had an appointment to meet.

Sneaking out the kitchen door, he hurried to Friedrich's side of the house, tapping lightly on the door.

"Are you ready?"

"I've got to ask permission. Don't forget your excuse."

It was not hard to get Friedrich's parents to say "yes," for they were used to the boys' evening frolics.

"Remember studies. Don't stay too long and don't go too far away."

The usual admonitions. Both boys knew them by heart. They wearied at the multiple demands of their mothers.

"Well, come on, Friedrich. What's wrong with you? Don't you know we have to hurry?"

"I had to fix something." Friedrich gave one sock a yank and limped forward on the other foot.

"Well, come on, let's go." Hansie had almost lost his nerve several times this evening. And then he would see his mother's face again, engraved with concern, and he would see in his mind's eye that huge pile of carrots, rotting away. Infuriated, he would blot out scary memories of Tante Anni's forced departure and stories he had heard about *them*. He would get some of those carrots

95

and no one would know the difference, or he'd know the reason why!

Again Hansie turned to the dawdling, stumbling Friedrich, disgusted at his impractical gawkiness.

"Sometimes I think you are so stupid, Friedrich, for as smart as you are in school. Now look, we'll have to hurry while we still have a little light to see where we are. We'll cut across here"—he motioned toward the adjacent field—"and go back through Herr Fetzer's sugarbeet field."

"Hans, do you really think we should? If we'd get caught, our folks would have to pay the consequences. And you know what they might be!"

"I thought it made you mad about the wasted carrots."

"Well, sure, but—"

"All right, so we're going to do something about it. We'll never get caught. Come on. Remember the rab—"

"Oh, have it your own way, then. But forget that rabbit, will you?"

"I will if you come on and stop being so stubborn."

Stealthily the two youngsters crept through the back field and wormed their way through the tall grasses adjoining the plot where the carrots had been piled in a heap. Only two hundred feet away protruded the large villa, center of authority for the village. Suddenly and without warning Hansie halted.

"What in the world, Hans? Why don't you tell a fellow?"

"Shhhh. We'd better not be too close together. I'll check to be sure no one is around. Then I'll make a dash and fill my sack. Then you come and fill yours. Then we run home as fast as we can, see? Don't wait for me. Just run. All right, I'm ready."

Friedrich groaned. A whole afternoon of misgivings had culminated in an ugly headache and a pain in his side. He wished he had not come. How he wished it, as he strained his eyes to see the last of the foolhardy Hans, braving forward with careful, mincing, but determined steps.

All of a sudden Friedrich heard something that almost paralyzed him until he got control of his senses and began to run. Like a bullet he beelined across the fields and toward home, every nerve in him pushing him faster. Never had he run so fast in his whole life.

Friedrich could not understand the language of the occupying army, but he didn't need an interpreter to translate the angry shouts he had heard behind him. Shouts aimed at his best friend, foolish friend that he was. Finally out of danger, Friedrich hid behind a pigsty. He cried like a baby.

"Please, please come, Hansie, hurry! Don't let them get you, please," he whispered aloud, wanting to pray but not knowing how to go about it.

And then, even before he got his prayer formulated, Friedrich's glad eyes beheld the answer, Hansie coming like an arrow from the north rather than from the west where Friedrich had looked for him, Hansie stumbling but regaining ground, Hansie sackless and carrotless like himself.

"Hans," he half whispered, half shouted. "Hans, here I am."

"Aren't you home yet? Don't stop. Run, I say!" Hansie ordered, gasping for breath and continuing his race with time.

"Did he see you?"

They stood, panting, in front of the house.

"Sure, he saw me." Hansie was whiter than Friedrich had ever seen him, and his eyes were filled with terror.

"We'd better go in. He didn't see *you;* so you just keep quiet about it. But I'll have to tell Grandpa."

He paused and the authority he had displayed fifteen minutes before had vanished. This time Hansie was scared.

"I'll have to tell Grandpa and Mamma. But you keep still about it."

"And so, my dear Maria," Grandpa was saying, as Hansie fell into the door, closing it quickly behind him, "you won't need to go. I think we can manage."

His words fell quietly over the small room, like soft snow on a peaceful winter scene. Mamma was seated in the rocker, her fingers busy mending Rosie's only dress. Rosie, clad in the night clothes Grandma had worked up for her from an old nightshirt of Grandpa's, lay curled up on the floor at her mother's feet. Grandma sat quietly, her hands motionless in her lap.

"But, Grandpa," Mamma started, "you must think of yourself. It's this way." Suddenly she glanced up and saw Hansie.

"Hans!"

He dropped on the floor beside Rosie, his outside body aching and his insides turning somersaults. He felt sick all over and every attempt at words brought unsolicited tears to his eyes and voice. Why had he done it? At any moment the door might open and they might all be arrested. He shuddered. He must tell them what he had done. But how could he?

And then he felt her hand on his shoulder, Mamma putting her arm around him, Mamma understanding. Somehow he did not rebel at it. There was no pride left in him at all.

It was then that he began to blurt out the story.

"Friedrich and I saw the—*their* carrot pile. He said last year they wasted them, they let them rot. It made me mad. With us having to leave and everything—" He stopped to sob. "Because we didn't have enough—to eat. I talked Friedrich into it—it wasn't his fault. We took our sacks. Grandpa's is still in the field where I dropped it."

He looked uncertainly at his mother. "It wouldn't have been stealing, because they waste them anyway."

"Go on with the story, Son."

He didn't want to tell the rest. At last he forced himself to do it.

"They didn't see Friedrich, but they did see me. He—he shouted at me and I ran."

"Who saw you?" This from Grandpa.

"The—the soldier." He hid his face to keep Grandpa from looking at him so hard.

"He chased me a little way, but I fooled him. I ran north a while back beyond Fetzers' field and then when I lost him I turned east. I—I think he gave up."

Somewhere in the back of his mind, Hansie had hoped that the family might comfort him with words of assurance, say it didn't matter, that the soldier wouldn't be able to find him, or some such thing. But they didn't.

Instead they all sat thinking, stunned by his story. Finally Grandpa spoke.

"Come here, Son," he said huskily.

"Do you think they will look for me?" Hans queried, seating himself beside Grandpa, but avoiding looking into his face.

"I don't think so. They have other things they would rather do in the evening. But if he got a good look at you, he may remember you when he sees you again. And that might be dangerous for all of us."

The old man hesitated for a minute, wondering if he should say more. Then he looked at Mamma, who was listening closely to every word.

"Last year a man did what Hansie tried this evening. They caught him."

"And what—?"

"They beat him and put him in a dark basement without food."

"Ohhhh." Maria wished that she had not urged him to go on. Rosie was deeply disturbed.

"As I said," Grandpa continued in his slow way, "they won't go out tonight looking for a slip of a boy. I hate to say this, Maria, but I believe you ought to leave."

"Should we leave tonight?"

"Wait until an hour or so before dawn." He stopped to give Grandma a reassuring look. She was crying.

"I can hardly stand to tell you to go, Maria, but it is for your own sakes."

"I know."

She thought a while. "But the trouble is, I don't know where to go from here."

"You know you want to go west, don't you?"

"Of course. But west is a big place."

Slowly and methodically Grandpa pulled himself to his feet and hobbled into the bedroom. When he came back, he carried an old, intricately carved chest in one hand and a key in the other. Checking to be sure that the shades were drawn, he sat down and looked wistfully at the family about him. What he said then was not easy for him. More than once he almost choked on the words.

"As you are all aware," he pronounced solemnly, as though he were beginning a formal speech, "Grandma and I are very old. We don't have very long to live, and we know it. Long ago we began saving for our grandchildren. Our grandchildren are gone. We cannot bring them back. But Hansie and Rosie have been grandchildren to us, and you, Maria, have been as a daughter. We can never repay you.

"Now, if you walk for an hour west of this town, you will come to Heuchlingen, where there is a railroad station. The trains do not run very regularly, but they do go west. We know these marks aren't worth very much today, but I think they will see you quite a distance along your way."

His fingers trembling, the old man counted out a pile of coins and some paper money. Then he lifted out a stack of papers precious to his family, and from them drew out a map of Germany.

"This may also be a real help to you. Maria, we knew that you would soon be leaving, in spite of the fact that we tried to keep you with us. That is why we have thought this through as completely as we have. You are not a well woman. Grandma and I have both noticed that you have been getting weaker as the summer wears

101

on, and that those dizzy spells come more frequently. You cannot stand to walk many miles again."

Maria dropped her head. The goodness of the old couple, their complete unselfishness, made her feel unworthy of their gifts.

He went on. "You may do as you wish, Maria, but when you get to Heuchlingen, before you take a train for anywhere, why don't you find out where another one of those hospitals is located? You know, like the one your husband took the baby to."

Maria raised her eyes and looked at the face of the man who spoke, and she felt warm toward him as though he were her father.

"But how can we take your life savings?"

Grandpa pretended gruffness.

"Don't be foolish. What can we do with it? Don't waste time being sentimental."

"But how will you get everything harvested and the winter's supply of wood without Hansie? I'm afraid for us to stay and yet I hate to go for fear of what will happen to you. You are so much like our own family."

She laid her hand on Grandma's.

"You've been so kind."

Grandpa coughed and looked away. "Since you have been talking of going, Maria, Grandma and I have done a lot of thinking. We can get some more help from youngsters like Friedrich next door in exchange for some of our milk. But there is something else, Maria, more important."

Grandma sat looking at Rosie, sitting cross-legged on the floor. "I guess God didn't mean very much to us before you came here, Maria. But you're always talking about

God caring for you, your faith and trust in Him, made us do some thinking, too."

"And so, Maria," Grandpa finished, "if you want to know how we'll get along without you, it will be hard. But the same God who looks after you will take care of us, too. We have learned to trust in Him, Maria, by watching the way you live."

13

IT WAS FALL: restless, frustrated weather, a moody north wind expressing its disquietude by tumbling the sensitive brown and golden leaves headlong to the ground, where they lay awaiting another sweep of wind or the rambunctious prancing of a squirrel. Maria sat on the sun porch of the Niederwinden Lutheran Hospital, where she had been for the past two months, watching Nature's little flurry, her thoughts as aimless as the irresponsible leaves. A bee, apparently aware that he was a trespasser on the sun porch, and wildly unhappy about his plight, flung his body against the pane, buzzing angrily.

Maria listened to the slow, even tempo of feet outside on the pavement. It was not the heavy, insistent clicking of men going to work, nor the uninhibited feet of school children, but the responsible, tired feet of housewives on the many errands of their day, to and fro in the little town. In an hour the monotonous plodding of the town women would give way to the shrill cries, teasing voices, singing, and blustering of the town's school children, homeward bound. Some of the more pale-faced ones would trudge along at the same dull tempo as their mothers, defeated beneath their heavy book bags.

Maria closed her eyes and wanted to be outside, out where the world smelled like life instead of medicine, where she could reach down and run her fingers through the good earth beneath her. She wanted to be out where the sky above her would stretch itself as a whole panorama of delicate clouds instead of being confined within the large glass panes of the sun porch.

Even more she longed to lead her children westward again, to walk where there were more faces to search, search with the hope of finding Hans. Almost seven months had passed; would a few more wrinkles enhance the dearness of that face? The feeling that Hans was alive—she could not believe otherwise—accelerated the beating of her heart and made her determined to get well.

Outside the rhythmic motion of the leaves, their grasp on the limbs becoming weaker, kept sway with Maria's thoughts. She closed her eyes and remembered her native home, now desecrated by war and plunderings. Was not each familiar tree still standing in its appointed place, where her great-great-grandfather had planted it? Did not the sparrows still flutter about the house and the berry bushes flourish to the west of the fence, even though house and barn were mutilated by unappreciative hands? If it were not for the unchanging quality of nature, and the unalterable personality of the One who had made it all, Maria knew that the insecurity of her existence as a refugee would be unbearable.

Wrapped up in her own little bundle of hopes and philosophies, Maria did not notice the sudden swish of starched uniform enter the room, nor did her ears catch the quick step of Sister Lisa, as she came over to her bed. Seeing that Maria was either sleeping or deep in thought, Sister Lisa paused, laying down the armful of freshly washed linen she carried and looking once more at the envelope, obviously a telegram, addressed to Frau Maria Penner.

"Maria."

She opened her eyes, startled not so much by the presence of the figure in starched blue as by the urgent way in which she had called her name.

"Maria, it is a telegram for you from the British Zone."

"For me? But why would I be getting a telegram?" Maria knew only one person in the British Zone, a cousin whose address she had suddenly recalled one day since she came to this hospital. She had written to this cousin and had received a letter in response, but that would not explain a telegram.

Hans! Could he be in the British Zone? But how would he know her whereabouts?

Maria snatched the envelope with trembling fingers and tried awkwardly to open it, the weight of her body propped hard on her elbow. She drank up the message quickly, as Hansie was apt to swallow his soup, and then she devoured its contents again. Not until she had read and reread it several times did the quiet figure beside her, now seated and gazing out the window, come back into focus.

"I can't understand this, Sister Lisa," she said at length. "Could we go down to your office and talk it over?"

Maria had been very tired and more than a little sick when she and the children had arrived on the train in Niederwinden. She did not know what would have happened to her had not the Lord, through Grandpa Maier, supplied her with train fare. The matron and head nurse of the hospital, pert little Sister Lisa, had seen her need of hospital care and after a doctor's examination had admitted her and placed the children in a home. Now, after several months of rest, Maria's step quickened and she did not find it too hard to keep in step with Sister Lisa.

The nurse seated herself behind her desk, motioning to Maria to take the chair before her.

"It's a telegram from Gronau, in the British Zone, signed by an organization called Mennonite Central Committee. I have told you, Sister Lisa, that I am a Mennonite from Russia, but I have never heard of this committee. This is the way the telegram reads: RUTH REMPEL KIEL [that's my cousin I have been writing to] CONCERNED ABOUT YOUR HEALTH STOP SUGGEST GO TO SCHNAITHEIM. What do you think this means?"

Sister Lisa thought for a long moment, then reached into the drawer of her desk for a map.

"Schnaitheim, you know, Maria, is only a few kilometers on the other side of the zonal border. Come here, and I will show you where it is. Since Niederwinden is about a half day's walk from the border, I would say that the distance from here to Schnaitheim is no more than thirty-five kilometers. It's not the distance that stands between you and getting to Schnaitheim."

"I know. It's getting across the border. But do you think there is a health resort there? Or could this be a trick?"

"Apparently, Maria, your friends are conniving to get you across the border. They are probably more concerned about your political 'health' than your physical health at the moment."

"Would you go, if you were me?"

Sister Lisa's face became grave.

"I'd hate to see you try it alone. People living close to the border tell me that they hear shots every day."

107

"Suppose I would try to beg my way across?"

The woman on the other side of the desk shook her head sadly.

"I don't think there's much use trying that. I think it would be a waste of time. A long walk with the children to no avail."

The mention of Hansie and Rosie reminded Maria of another matter that she had been wondering about. More than once she had approached Sister Lisa about the children in the past few days, but each time the nurse had carefully evaded her questions.

"Sister Lisa, when do you think the children will come in again? They haven't been to see me for days."

Sister Lisa was usually imperturbable, master of any situation. From the well-tied bow on her worn but proud-faced shoes to the pert white bow tied crisply beneath her chin, she was an expert in managing her own well-disciplined life and in bringing other people's consciences in line with her own strict one. But Sister Lisa made a poor hypocrite; her usually crisp voice was suddenly undignified and scratchy.

"Maria, you can't expect the children to come in every day. If Frau Lucke is going to take care of them, she deserves their help in the afternoon. And the evenings get dark sooner. You wouldn't want them coming up here after dark."

Maria still held the telegram tightly in her hand. Her dark eyes searched the face of her friend.

"Sister Lisa, are those children all right? You're holding something back from me, aren't you?"

The slim figure was now making its busy way around the room, tidying up an already meticulous table, stacking up some books on one side of her desk, throwing a few scraps of paper into the wastebasket. Realizing that she could no longer procrastinate, Lisa turned quickly around to face Maria. Her voice was penitent.

"I'm sorry, Maria. Frau Lucke has found her food supply getting so meager that the children have not been eating enough to send them to school. It is the same problem everywhere, they talk of closing the schools. Yet for those who can go, it is a God-given release."

"Then Hans and Rosie are sick from undernourishment?"

"Not exactly sick, but weak. Frau Lucke was here this morning and I slipped her a few potatoes from our hospital supply." The nurse leaned forward, continuing in a confidential tone. "I shouldn't have done it—it's against rules—but I felt I had to."

Glancing at her watch, Sister Lisa rose.

"Don't worry about the children, Maria. Talk to the heavenly Father about it, and read the Bible which I gave you. Forget the telegram, at least for the present."

Thoughtfully Maria returned to her room and crawled into bed, where she lay staring out the window without really seeing anything in the landscape before her, not even the children now coming from school. Why watch them if Rosie and Hans were not along?

Could it be that her children's need for food and this strange telegram came at the same time for a purpose? Was she well enough to consider making another journey westward?

One question confronted Maria above all others, as she turned her problem over in her mind. Could she and the children get across the border safely into the British

Zone? Every refugee knew how carefully international borders were guarded, how signs of warning, armed policemen, electrified barbed wire, and well-trained dogs were ever on hand to prevent illegal crossing. With no knowledge of the surrounding countryside, it would be suicide for her to try to sneak across "black." The only other alternative, that of begging her way across, also had its risks, for there was the constant danger of Communist soldiers discovering her nationality and sending her back to Russia again, as they had Tante Anni and so many others like her. Some people tried bribing border officials with food or cigarettes, but that, too, was impossible for Maria.

It was then that she took her Bible from the stand beside her bed. Ever since Sister Lisa had sensed her deep longing for a Bible and had given her one, she had never missed reading it.

"Lord, give me a watchword," she prayed, as she opened to the Book of Joshua, where she had stopped the day before. Yesterday she had read the first chapter, but now she had a deep urge to read the passage again. For she remembered how the words of God to Joshua had comforted her:

> Be strong and of a good courage:
> be not afraid, neither be thou dismayed:
> for the Lord thy God is with thee whithersover thou
>   goest.

She scanned the passage until she found that verse again. There was no use reading further; she couldn't think about anything but the problem at hand. And, after all, what more did she need than those words? Had not God's presence been very real to her ever since the miracle of Stony City?

For a long time she prayed, while the shadows deepened and the Lord threw His protecting cloak of darkness over the land. The nurses brought in hot cereal for supper, and once Sister Lisa stopped for a quick checkup of her patient. Maria motioned her over to the bed, placing her hand upon the thin white arm.

"I want you to send a telegram for me, Sister Lisa," she said quietly. "I have spoken to the Lord, and I think He has spoken to me. I have a strong urge that we should try going by way of the border officials."

She ignored the puzzled look on the face of her friend.

Sister Lisa wrote the message on a slip of paper, then stood frowning as she reread it.

TO THE MENNONITE CENTRAL COMMITTEE
GRONAU
GERMANY

PLANNING TO MAKE TRIP FOR HEALTH AS SUGGESTED STOP
CAN WE MEET AT TRAIN STATION NIGHT OF OCTOBER 10

MARIA PENNER

Suddenly a look of frank admiration came into her eyes. "It is very well worded," she whispered. "The train station is always good place to wait. And I don't believe that this telegram will throw any suspicion on you. If you can only make it across the border, everything will be all right."

111

14

SISTER LISA had never looked so lovable as she did that morning when she helped Maria fasten her bundle once more upon her back. The wiry Hans was difficult to hitch, but Lisa, every hair in its appointed place, seemed scarcely to know that it was only five in the morning as she wrestled to get Hans' bundle "just right" to suit him. Maria noticed that she was briskly efficient, even though her demeanor was softened by the parting moment and her eyes were misty.

They stood there for a long minute, their hands clasped in silent expression of their friendship, both stumbling to find words for their farewell. Maria remembered too plainly how near the end of her string she had been when they stumbled into the door of the Lutheran Hospital, and she remembered Hansie saying, "I do believe Sister Lisa likes us, Mamma."

Lisa had loved them, along with all her other patients, and she had made the same sacrifices for them that she had made for the others. But it was more than a nurse-patient relationship, for Sister Lisa and Maria were both Christians and their faith kept them spiritually above their oft-despairing fellow men.

"You might never see us again, Sister Lisa, but on the other hand, you might find us returned to your doorstep in a few hours."

The thought was not humorous and frightened her a bit, but there was a look of confidence on Lisa's face.

112

"God still works miracles, Maria. We will pray."

"I can't thank you enough—"

"It is I who am indebted. Helping you was my professional duty—I vowed it—but it was a lasting satisfaction and pleasure as well."

She paused for a moment to kiss Rosie and give her brother a brief hug.

"You know, Maria, we sisters don't have children of our own, but young ones like Hans and Rosie are in a sense ours, too. Knowing them compensates."

They smiled at one another in the dim light of the early morning. Then Rosie curtsied, Hansie bowed, and Maria murmured a "Many, many thanks." Turning, she led the children down the path and onto the road. Lisa followed them to the end of the path and waved at them as, every few yards, they turned and waved again to her.

When they were so far from the hospital that only the hedge could be seen, Maria realized that Sister Lisa was already busy on her morning rounds and that young nurses would soon be scurrying to give breakfasts and baths. And all the while Lisa would be praying for her and her children. Busy as she was, she would slip into her study and have her quiet time with God.

It was strange, Maria thought, strange and providential, how the Lord brought them from one oasis of friendship to another through the vast desert of their homeless existence. She squeezed Rosie's hand and remembered Lisa's parting advice to start out at a slow, even pace.

Quietly they padded through the dozing bourg, gazing blankly at the empty shop windows and the closed shutters of the village bedrooms. When they came to the bakeshop, Maria noticed Hansie survey its empty display shelves with contempt.

"How long did you have to wait for your ration this week?" she asked kindly. It had seemed very long since they had had a really good chat, just the three of them.

"We never got it, Mamma. We were going to come up and talk to you about it, but Sister Lisa wouldn't let us."

"I know, she was afraid it would worry me. But you might as well tell me the whole story now."

"Well," Hansie began, "Sister Lisa, she's all right, I guess, but when I wanted to tell you what happened in the bread line, she sent us both home. We felt terrible."

"But the next day she was nice again," Rosie added, her grievance now healed. "She gave us some broth to take home to Frau Lucke because we didn't have any bread ration."

"But why didn't you get it?" Maria wanted to know. "You didn't get too hungry this week, did you?"

"I guess we would have, if it hadn't been for Sister Lisa. You see, Mamma, Rosie and I were taking turns standing in line. It still makes me mad; I'd like to knock a couple of———guys down."

"Hans! Hansie Penner, where did you hear such language?"

"All the other fellows on our street say it."

"That doesn't make it right. But finish telling your story."

"I got there real early, Mom, and didn't go to school so we could get our ration. Frau Lucke didn't feel well enough to wait in line. I stood all the morning until I was so tired I wasn't hungry any more, and then Rosie

114

came to stand a while. People kept crowding in ahead of Rosie and me, just because they were grown and could get by with it. Then one man saw how they treated us and started an argument with another man—"

"The other man had slapped me, Mamma," Rosie added.

Hansie flushed and continued. "Then the tall man who had slapped Rosie told the other fellow that if he wanted to fight about it, he could step out of the line. The other man stepped out and the one who said it didn't. Then the people began to scream because they were fighting right there in the line, and a woman behind Rosie fainted, and the policeman came up and hauled them both away."

"Yes, and then the man in the store, the baker, came out and said he was sorry, but the bread was all gone."

"Oh, children, was it really that bad?" Maria's heart ached for them. She wondered what else had gone on that they had never had a chance to tell her.

They continued their walking steadily, ceased conversing because it tired them, and soon realized that they were only a short distance from the border. Just how long they had walked they did not know. But Maria judged they were nearing their destination when they began seeing people, refugees like themselves, coming from the opposite direction, disappointment written strong upon their faces.

"It's no use," a tired old woman confided in them, as they stopped for a moment to rest. "I just came from there myself. I guess I've tried to cross that way just about as often as I'm going to. Wouldn't be afraid to sneak across through the forest, but my son on the other side begged me never to do it."

"But you are going to try anyway?" Maria asked.

"If I live, I am." The old woman's voice trembled. "I've got connections. If I can just get some produce from a farmer, or a few packages of cigarettes, I can get all the help I need."

She cocked her head to one side and gave them one last, scrutinizing look. "I wouldn't bother those officials if I were you. It's just no use."

Maria gave the children a little hinting push. It was time to get away from the pessimistic old woman. She dared not forget her watchword, *Be strong and of a good courage . . . the Lord thy God is with thee . . . .*

"Good-bye, God bless you," she said over her shoulder.

The man who next appeared around the corner was no more assuring than the woman had been.

"There are at least six patrols along this road, lady. With those youngsters, you'd better watch out."

"German?" The knowing half-grin on his face shamed Maria. She hadn't meant to display her apprehension to a stranger, but she did want to know.

"The Russians aren't on duty, if that's what you meant. They let the Germans do most of the work. But it doesn't hurt to be careful, lady."

Again Maria found herself quickening her pace, scurrying along almost too fast for Rosie. However this ordeal would turn out, Maria wanted to get it over with. She set her face toward the west with even more determination.

Hansie caught her spirit. "I'm not afraid of *them*,"

he declared. And then he remembered the carrots. "That is, when *they're* not chasing me with a club."

Suddenly he stopped in his tracks. Maria saw what he had seen, and she too stopped.

"An auto, Mamma!" Hansie cried. "There's an auto coming." Rosie moved close to Maria.

The Lord . . . is with thee whithersoever thou goest.

Announcing its coming with a whirl of dust and a purr of motor, a little *Volkswagen* drew up beside the party and an officer hopped out. At least the color of his uniform was green, Maria noticed immediately, and not a gray-blue. The lines in his face were hard, however, and he gazed at them with professional disinterest. Rosie was crying and Hansie looked on with a mixture of fear and awe.

"Where do you think you are going?" The officer's words lashed out at them, and Maria suddenly felt like a foolish child attempting some ridiculous prank. The speech she had been preparing completely left her, and at that moment she would have fallen at the man's feet, if it would have helped, to make him understand how desperate her need was.

Be not afraid . . . for the Lord thy God is with thee . . . .

It wasn't what she had planned to say, but it was the only thing her choked-up voice could stammer out.

"Please, sir, won't you have a heart?"

The man glanced down at the beseeching faces of the children and at the soft, wet face of the refugee woman, amazingly trustful for one in her circumstances. Maybe he thought of his own children at home, or maybe he wondered at the boldness of the woman to make the

117

request, or maybe he was just tired of turning people back. He shrugged his shoulders and got back into the *Volkswagen* again, slamming the door behind him.

"All right. Go on." The sound of his voice died out in the noise of the motor, and he was gone.

Maria could have wept. She felt like stopping right there in the middle of the road and kneeling in thanksgiving, but she knew they must hurry on. Hansie watched the auto disappear down the road.

"He let us go, Mamma!" he shouted. "He didn't turn us back."

Maria smiled through her tears. "But there will be more. Let's—"

"O God," she suddenly prayed. "There comes another one."

The man in the uniform walked up to them brusquely. He was large and he looked down his nose at them with impatience and contempt. It was obvious that they were another intrusion in his day.

"And where are you going?" he asked.

I will go with thee whithersoever thou goest.

The words that had worked the other time came to Maria again. She could not have said them more humbly.

"Please, sir, won't you have a heart?"

He avoided her eyes when he answered them.

"Get going," he barked. "But hurry up before you get me into trouble." With that he snapped back into his uniformed world, clicking his heels to keep from appearing soft. When his uniform disappeared down the road, Maria let out the breath she had been holding.

"O God," she muttered, "don't let me down; don't let me doubt. We've got to get through."

Maria never could explain it, the miracle of her border crossing. She told it many times afterward, for it was the crowning chapter of the whole story of her escape to safety under the care of God. People later opened their mouths and stared at her in amazement, some frankly doubted her word, but it was true, real-life truth, stranger than fiction. For the bedraggled little group met three policemen before they breathed the air of safety, and every one of the officers waved them on in answer to Maria's simple plea, "Please have a heart." It was as though the Lord struck them with a temporary paralysis, as though they were unable to touch her.

Probably the last officer, the one at the border itself, was the toughest. So vital it was that he give his permission that Maria shook in her thin shoes. Her whole body ached by that time and the children were fidgety. Her faith almost gave way at the sight of that last broad green uniform, topped with a burly head. She tried not to see the sardonic grin and the snapping eyes. Almost she would have preferred to brave the dangers of crossing through the woods to the psychological gunfire of that face.

Be not afraid . . . the Lord thy God . . . .

"A heart, lady?" The officer burst into a guffaw. "What's that? I stopped having a heart long ago in this business!" After all, they had *no* papers, no papers at all, to insure their crossing the Great Divide.

There was a long pause in which her eyes had implored him, and then it happened again.

"Get your ——— kids and get out of here before you get me in trouble. And keep your mouth shut about it, see?"

Gratefully Maria nodded and, almost running, led the children out of the little wooden shanty, past the red flag, and under the roadblock. Swiftly they went, for their lives depended upon it, yet not too swiftly lest they appear too anxious and the officer suddenly change his mind.

They didn't look back, for they wanted no last look. Hurrying through the little town which first greeted them, regarding people only as necessary obstacles to their path, they soon found themselves off the main road and past the sign pointing to their destination.

Maria was glad that she had allowed an extra day to get to the train station in Schnaitheim, for they had not made very good time today so far as speed in walking was concerned. But it did not matter. Nothing mattered except that they had crossed over into the British Zone, the most formidable hurdle of their journey westward.

And there, in the fast falling dusk of the evening, the little group slipped off the road to erect an altar in their hearts to the Lord, who had brought them through the "Red Sea" to freedom. But Maria did not finish that prayer without beseeching God for the safety of Hans, who so far as she knew, still remained behind the Iron Curtain that separated the East and West Zones of postwar Germany.

15

It was morning when the little red pickup truck, which brought the Penner family from the railroad station in Schnaitheim to the Mennonite camp at Gronau, arrived at its destination. Maria was soon to learn that Schnaitheim was only a meeting place, that Gronau was where they were going.

Enough light had trickled from the heavens to show up the outlines of the crooked old buildings hunched close to the winding streets of Gronau, but it was still early enough that the shutters were closed over the windows and the quiet town was lifeless.

Although Gronau was situated within two miles of the Dutch-German border, although the Netherlands lay only a short stretch westward, the shop windows that bordered the streets were just as sadly empty as all the other store windows in postwar Germany. Holland had begun to get back on her feet, and her stores were now laden with plenty, but the border between the two countries was impassable.

Maria, worn out from the strain and excitement of the past few days and now able to relax as a result of the new freedom from fear, slept during most of the journey. Hansie was securely fastened between the driver and Maria, and Rosie snuggled in her mother's lap. Only one thought marred Maria's complete enjoyment of the trip to camp: if only Hans, Big Hans, could share her fortune!

121

For the first hour they had talked, the driver, Wladimir Klassen, describing the camp in which he had found refuge and the kindness of the American Mennonites who had come to establish this temporary home for their people. They had talked of their homeland, their trek, their predicament as unwanted people, until Maria, in spite of her interest in their conversation, could no longer keep awake. Every now and then she woke up to view another mangled town, dismally void of signs of life, a few scattered street lights revealing the tragedy that had taken place only a few short years before. Bricks and rubble lay everywhere; twisted, gnarled steelwork wrapped itself about tumble-down walls. It was an old sight to Maria; she gladly closed her eyes to the disfigured landscape and dozed again.

And so it was that now, after several hours of driving through peaceful countryside and bombed-out towns, they finally pulled up in front of a large villa, set back discreetly from the road behind a heavy iron gate. Maria sat up with a start, suddenly aware that driver Klassen had pulled the brake and was climbing out of his side of the truck. Smiling, he came around to the other side, opening the door for her and helping her out.

"This is the headquarters building," he informed her, pointing beyond a simple wooden sign which read in bold, black letters, "Mennonite Central Committee of the United States and Canada."

"This is where the main offices and the hospital rooms for the camp are, and since no one is up at the *Lager* yet, Frau Director has asked me to give you a bed here until later in the morning."

He lifted Rosie from her lap and gave Maria his arm.

Maria had not realized how exhausted she was in mind and body until she climbed from the pickup, stretched, and looked about her. The long kilometers she had walked, the privation she had endured, the strain from all the uncertainty of her life, the absence of her loved ones, all these things had sapped her strength and made her chronically ill. As she leaned upon Herr Klassen's arm for support, she was aware that a hospital bed was not amiss for her. For one frightening moment the villa, the red truck, the iron fence, trees, ground, and sidewalk swirled before her eyes.

After that she was admitted to camp, assigned her bed, and cared for without even finding it out. And when she awoke, it was no longer morning.

"Frau Penner." The voice came from a clean young face, leaning sympathetically over her bed. "The journey is over, Frau Penner, and you are here at Gronau, safe. Can't you take a bit of nourishment? Perhaps this soup will help."

Maria looked at the woman in the freshly laundered uniform. She glanced at the other beds in the room, replete with mattresses and sheets. Sunshine blessed her from the window. And the words that were directed to her were spoken in *Plattdeutsch,* the beloved dialect of her people. She took a sip of the pungent-smelling soup extended toward her.

"Safe?" She wiped the tears that marred her view of the face; she liked the strength of it. To her surprise the bright eyes above the bowl also filled with tears.

"Yes, Frau Penner, safe among friends."

"But Hansie, and Rosie. Where are they?" She sat up in bed, then lay back against the pillows, looking squarely at the girl. "I left them with the driver, Herr Klassen. Did they also get soup? I can't eat if they're hungry—"

"It's all right, Frau Penner. They were fed this morning when you arrived, and again at noon, and soon they will be given their supper. You were too weak, too tired, even to eat. After you have eaten this soup and bun, the doctor will come in to examine you, and then the children will be brought up before they are put to bed."

Then the children were safe. She was safe.

. . . the Lord thy God will be with thee, whithersover thou goest.

"He was with me," she murmured. She did not eat the bun, but lay back again, falling into another deep sleep.

Maria would always remember that evening. The children, fed, rested, bathed, and dressed in warm new clothes, stood by her bedside, chattering about the room they shared with another small family—a room separated from their neighbors by blanket walls. Hansie told her of the many people he had seen in the camp, the little boy that lived in their room, the soup line he had stood in, and many other details that had impressed his mind. Rosie displayed her new clothes that the *nice* lady had given her, and insisted that Hansie hold up his foot so that Mamma could see the splendid socks that he was wearing. And the shoes! Hans blinked back the tears when he showed his mother the shoes, so well-fitting, so long overdue.

Actually Maria heard very little of what the children said as they leaned over her bed, their faces hungry for her companionship, their hands lovingly touching hers above the sheets. She knew only that her children were finally being cared for in a way that she, their mother, had longed to do for many years.

It was then that they heard heavy footsteps come down the hall and looking up, saw a young man enter the room. Tall and broad-shouldered, he had an air of confidence about him.

"I represent the Mennonite Central Committee, and I believe you are Frau Penner," he said in easy-flowing *Platt.* "We are so happy that you arrived safely." And she knew from the way he said it that he meant it.

"When you are feeling better I'll want to hear all about your trip and many other things. But in the meantime, the doctor says that you are to take it pretty easy for a while. How do you feel this evening?"

"Much, much better," Maria answered with difficulty, trying to swallow the lump in her throat. "You are so very kind. I don't know how to thank you."

"God has been good to us in Canada. My parents made the long trip from Russia after the revolution in 1925. I was only five then, but I can still remember a little about the trip. We who have been so blessed ourselves have a debt to pay to our brethren. Our only desire is to help as many of our brothers and sisters as we possibly can." He spoke with conviction.

"But—but how did you in Canada, so far away, find out about us?"

The young man frowned, formulating his reply; then his face brightened.

"As I said, Frau Penner, we have been greatly blessed in the United States and Canada. Most of us are far from rich, but we are not in need. Our homes have not been destroyed nor our loved ones taken from us. Maybe the emblem on my sleeve will help me tell the story."

Hansie, who had been listening to the new friend with keen interest, moved closer to see the colorful emblem which was sewed neatly on the sleeve of his gray suit.

They noticed a cross embroidered in yellow against a red background, encircled by the words, "Mennonite Central Committee Relief." In the foreground were two hands clasped in a warm handshake.

"Because of the love of God for us, because of His gift to us in the person of Jesus Christ," he continued, "we Mennonites in America united to give help and relief to those whose lives were disrupted in the past dreadful war. We give this witness to everyone in need, regardless of race or creed. But we did not dream that we would discover thousands of our own brethren-in-the-faith scattered and stranded throughout western Europe. How we thank God every day that we can help them, too! It is truly an act of God's hand; we deserve no credit."

"But you will be rewarded." There was much more that Maria longed to say, but the wonder of God's providence saturated her being and made talking impossible.

The young man smiled. "We are being rewarded now, more than you can know and far more than we deserve."

He rose to go. "I think I'd better take the children back to their room at the *Lager* now. You need rest."

Obediently Hansie strode over to the man and stood waiting to return to his new home. But Rosie, stifling a sob, threw herself against her mother and buried her face in the sheet.

126

"Rosie, dear, what is wrong? We're here with friends, safe at last, and a warm bed is waiting for you."

How much better that would be, she thought, than the unfriendly, hard cement floor that had been the children's bed last night in the Schnaitheim train station!

"I want to ask you just one thing before we go, Mamma," Rosie finally answered when she recovered her voice.

"Is it really true that—that we don't need to be afraid any more?"

16

MARIA GAVE THE THIRD COT a gentle pat and stood back to observe the room. Everything was in order: beds were made, clothes hung neatly, the rough table and the only chair dusted, and Rosie's little bouquet of wild flowers nicely arranged in the center of the table. Now if they could just make something pretty to put on that wall; let's see—

Maybe she had better rest before the children came in from doing their morning exercises, or she wouldn't be able to go with them on that tour she had promised. She had no idea she would get so tired from doing so little; why, nothing more than making the beds and tidying up their little cubicle had left her almost shaky. Small wonder the camp doctor had decreed that she rest the first week out of the hospital.

"After all you went through before you came to camp here at Gronau, and after lying in bed six months, you'd better take it a little easy for a while, or you'll be right back in this sick ward," he had commanded sternly, then softened the order with characteristic humor. "We don't want you back again—there aren't enough beds."

"But idle hands are the devil's workshop," she had objected.

"I don't think the devil would get much done if he had to depend on your workshop," the doctor had shot back at her. "Besides, if you run out of things to do for your own little ones, there are a nestful of motherless souls down the corridor from you, Herr Fast's children. And there are some older ladies who need someone to talk to. But now mind you, don't overdo even visiting for the first week."

She had promised that she wouldn't, for the privilege of being with her children again was one which she had no intention of forfeiting. It had been hard staying in bed those first six months after they had arrived in Gronau, trying to recuperate from her run-down condition, seeing the children only once a day when they came home from school.

And what had been still harder was the fact that the MCC (Mennonite Central Committee) workers had been unable to locate Hans, even though they had found many other Mennonites, scattered throughout western Germany, since Maria had come to camp. Periodically Maria had sent the children to the office to check, but the answer was always the same.

But yesterday was a day none of them would ever forget, for Maria had been officially released from the hospital and outfitted with new clothes from the MCC. With a little assistance, she had actually walked "home."

"Come on, Mamma, hurry, or we won't have time to get all around before study hour." It was Hansie whose voice broke into Maria's thoughts. Looking up, she saw the children push excitedly through the blanket door into their room. They each grabbed an arm, almost lifting her off her feet.

The little blanket-enclosed space in which the Penners lived was only one of many such tiny rooms in the auditorium-sized *Klubhaus,* a large dingy building once used by the town people for a recreational hall. In order to give each refugee family a bit of privacy, the MCC had partitioned these cubicles by hanging blankets over strung-up wires. Maria had been given a quota of four blankets for each member of her family, enough to partition off their area from the rest and to make a cot for each of them. A network of convenient pathways, forming little streets, zigzagged through the maze of family units. The refugees had named each so-called "street" after an MCC worker or some other person in camp whom they respected.

The children raced eagerly ahead, waiting now and then for Maria's slow legs to catch up. They had so many things to show her: the kitchen, the laundry, the shoemaker's shop, the shower room. They paused for a moment outside the veranda to watch a group of mothers settle around tubs of water to peel potatoes, visiting together as they worked. Children chased one another across the bare space that was their only playground, bent on having a little last-minute fun before their mothers would usher them into their rooms for morning study. Everywhere they went a pleasant hum of voices and signs of early-morning industry mixed with the delightful April sunshine.

At last they had seen almost everything and, circling the *Klubhaus,* they entered the front door. Maria was glad the tour was over; it was time for her to get off her feet.

"But we didn't show Mother the window where we get our rations or the office upstairs where we get our identification card," Rosie exclaimed, disappointed.

"It's time Mamma gets back to bed," Hansie ordered, and Maria looked at him with fresh surprise.

She sighed as she stretched out on the bottom cot they had designated for her. "Now, children, it's just about nine o'clock and time for study. If you need any drinks of water, Hansie, go and get them now."

She had heard complaints, while she lay in bed, about Hansie. Sometimes he was seen dashing around the halls during study hours. Of course, after questioning him, she would always be assured that he had been on some important errand.

The children sat down at the table and spread out their few materials: a Testament, a pencil, and a notebook for each child. Because there was no paper available for correction and reprint of textbooks written during the Hitler regime, all of the schools had to get along without textbooks until the 1948 currency reform. Thus, assignments were carefully copied by the students in their notebooks. Hansie was working at his arithmetic problems; Rosie painstakingly copied a verse from her Testament.

"Now where did you say you got those lovely Testaments?" Maria whispered, for she was fast learning that anything above a whisper was easily overheard.

"Some Sunday school class in Canada sent them, Mamma."

"From our dear brothers and sisters in the Lord, our teacher told us." Rosie's voice rose louder than it should have, and Maria held a finger to her lips.

"Do you think we'll hear from our relatives in Canada sometime like the Edigers did, Mom?" Rosie lowered her voice, fiddling with her braid and looking wistful.

"They got a box, and Rita told me that it had all kinds of things, chocolate and a dress for her and some coffee that **Rita's mom** traded downtown for a pair of glasses. Oh, my, I wish *our* relatives would send us a box."

"Shh." Maria felt ashamed. "Don't let anyone hear you talk like that. As though God hasn't been good enough to us, to bring us here, to make me well, and to give us such beautiful clothes. Shame on you, Rosie!"

"Yes, you *ought* to be ashamed. Don't let us hear you say anything like that again."

"You stop telling me what to do."

"Children!"

How long Maria slept she didn't know, but when she got awake, Hansie had gone to wash for dinner. Maria walked toward the women's washroom, feeling respectable again, like a real mother in a real home. She looked down and fingered the lovely print dress which had come in with a shipment of clothing from America and which had been fitted on her only yesterday. What an improvement it was over the hospital gowns she had had to wear so long!

"God bless whoever sent this dress," she murmured, wondering what the donor looked like and whether she was rich or had given out of the little that she had.

"Oops! Oh, I'm sorry, lady; I didn't see you coming around that corner."

"That's all right. I wasn't looking where I was going. I guess I was daydreaming."

She stared at the young man who was bowing and making apologies for running into her. That face—wasn't that the same boy who had reminded her of someone before? Who did he resemble? And why did he look at her so oddly and then turn away, as if he almost recognized her, too?

Should she call him back? Apologies made, he had turned to go again.

"Just a minute, son. Would you mind if I ask you who you are? You look so familiar."

"You mean you felt that way, too?" He laughed. "My name's Franz Gaeddert and I'm from Alexanderwohl."

She felt her eyes filling with tears. Then it was Gisela's son. "Your mother was Gisela Hiebert Gaeddert? Do you remember her cousin, Maria Penner, or were you too young to remember?"

He laid his hand on her arm. "Cousin Maria, of course I do. I'm on my way back to the factory now, but I'll drop in this evening for a chat. Tell you what, I'll bring my supper over and eat it with you."

"How wonderful! But Franz—" She hesitated, but she had to ask. "Just one thing more. Are any of your folks —alive?"

The boy kicked an imaginary something with his foot and tried to give the information as he would cold statistics.

"Mom, Siberia; Dad died before I left; sister Elisabeth married, widowed, and now in the MCC camp in Backnang. She might come here later. The rest—well, you know the story. Only God knows where they are."

Their eyes locked for what seemed a very long moment. Then, embarrassed, the boy turned to go.

"I do hope Elisabeth can come."

"So do I." He grinned. "Don't forget—company for supper."

She watched him hurry down the narrow aisle, one hand in his pocket, his tall, rather sturdy frame seemingly confident. He had a way about him that gave you the impression he was very sure of himself, almost indifferent to the tragedies that made up his past. But in that moment when the years had been bridged and understanding built up between them, Maria had seen the same frightened little boy she had known only a few years before. How strange it was that she hadn't known him at first sight, that day he had looked into her hospital room!

Trouble might come double, but blessings do, too, Maria thought, as she gathered up her dinnerware and joined her children in the line. She still had not gotten over the surprise of finding Elfrieda, a charming girl who had also received spiritual help from the minister at Stony City. Elfrieda was doing stenographic work in the immigration office of the MCC.

Now Franz had made complete her first day out of the hospital, for he, too, was a human tie between her old world and her new. Hansie needed the companionship of an older boy, and she needed the reassurance of Franz' smiling personality. But more than anything else, Franz symbolized to Maria hope, the hope of finding someone far dearer to her than her cousin's son.

children and divided out the evening portions of bread and cheese. Franz had brought along his own dry rations.

"How old are you now, Franz? Why, I don't think you were any older than our Hansie when I saw you last." She could still see the barefoot boy coming in from milking. The face was the same, except that the eyes looked wiser and experience had penciled a few thin lines across his forehead.

"Twenty."

"It hardly seems possible."

She stole a quick glance at his face again, noting a slight scar on the cheek that wasn't there when she had known him before, noticing also the clean blue shirt, open at the neck, and the dark, slicked-down hair.

"A lot of things have happened for all of us since that time." He quickly changed the subject. "You just got out of the hospital, didn't you?"

"Yes, this is the first supper I'm eating with the children. You're helping us celebrate. I can't describe how I feel—like a bird out of a cage, or something. I wish I were a poet; I'd like to write it down."

"I know how you feel."

"Were you in bed for a long time once?" Rosie wanted to know.

"It was worse than being in bed. I was prisoner of war for two years."

"What was that like?" Hansie was sitting next to Franz, watching him with admiration.

Franz looked at Maria and decided not to go into detail. "Oh, it wasn't so very nice. I felt like a bird out of a cage, too, when I got out. But let's talk about something else. What class are you in at school, Hans?"

137

"Just the fifth," Hansie replied, studying his plate soberly. "If we hadn't had to stop school so often, I could be in the seventh."

"Yes, I know all about that," Franz said sympathetically. "My school days stopped long before they should have. But you just work hard, Hans, and you'll catch up."

"Now that I'm home," Maria heard herself say, "I can start helping Hansie more with his work, and Rosie, too. Camp life is far from normal, but just being with the children is so wonderful."

From there the conversation went to matters of interest to Rosie and Hans, subjects which Franz introduced and carried along with enthusiasm. He seemed to be enjoying himself, Maria mused, as she sat back resting and listening, trying to catch up with the activities and thoughts of her children. How fine it would be to have a man in Hansie's life!

She hated to interrupt, but the clatter of dishes in the neighboring rooms had ceased. Everywhere people were hurrying to the dishwashing room, each person washing his own or his family's dishes in the huge kettle of steaming water.

"Rosie and Hans, won't you go and wash the dishes as you did this noon?" Maria suggested gently.

"Oh, Mom, couldn't Rosie do it by herself? I went for the supper."

"No, I think you'd better do it together."

"But when we finally get our turn in the long line and get back, it will be time to go to bed," Hansie objected again.

"We'll see lots more of each other, fellow," Franz assured him. "I was wondering if you wouldn't take a hike with me tomorrow after school."

"I surely would!" Hansie's eyes gleamed as he and Rosie disappeared with the carefully stacked dishes.

Maria watched them go to be sure they were really gone, then closed the curtain and sat down across from Franz.

"Now, Franz, while the children are gone, I'll tell you a little about us, and then I want to know what brought you here."

In a few words Maria summarized her story, describing briefly her trek, her reunion with and loss of Hans, Lenie's death, crossing the border, and the truck ride to safety at Gronau.

"And, Franz, I give God the glory for it all. Why didn't we share the fate of Tante Anni?" She shook her head. "God must have had a purpose, that's all I can figure out.

"But you, Franz, tell me your story, quickly before the children come back."

"It's much the same as yours, Cousin Maria, up to the day Mother disappeared in Poland. Elisabeth and Mother and I stayed together as long as we could, but you know how it was. We always had too much food to die, but not really enough to live. Finally Elisabeth and I just had to look for work. She was twenty and I was sixteen at the time. That was while the Germans were still occupying Poland. We found jobs within fifty miles of Mother. Then one day when I came home from work, there was a letter for me. Report to the German *Wehrmacht,* or pay the death penalty. I reported.

"I kept in touch with Mother and Elisabeth even after

we were forced back to Germany. But soon after the Russians came into Poland, Elisabeth went to visit Mother, and she was gone. She would not have gone off without giving us word, unless *one* thing had happened. Elisabeth searched for days, but there was no trace of her any place.

"Toward the end of the war the Germans got less choosy about age and experience requirements for their Secret Service men. One day, without asking any opinions from me, they gave me orders to transfer to the *S.S.* My commanding officer liked my looks; I was quite a bit huskier than I am now and they liked my big build."

Franz stopped and looked at Maria strangely. "I've got the *S.S.* blood type mark, Maria, on my arm. It might mean that I can't emigrate to Canada as a lot of the fellows are doing."

He whispered it, and Maria nodded understandingly. It was not something people liked to talk about.

"I guess your work in the *S.S.* was pretty unpleasant, wasn't it, Franz?" she asked.

"It seemed adventuresome to a lot of young men, but some of the things we had to do were Hell on earth, Maria. I'm sure you've seen enough horrors that I don't have to add to your collection.

"When the war ended in May of 1945, I was fortunately sent to an American prisoner-of-war camp. I say fortunately, because when I went through Berlin I saw a good many prisoners of war from Russia returning to their families, and I don't covet their experiences."

Maria knew what he meant, for she, too, had seen a few of them.

"I remember a man searching for his wife and two

children in Berlin," Franz continued. "If he ever found her, she must have had a terrible shock because he went away from home strong and healthy and returned a physical and mental wreck. He needed two canes to hobble on; his trousers scarcely held together.

"I saw another one lying in a ditch. A group of people were standing watching him. Curiosity got the best of all of us and we stopped to look. His leg was bloody and he was a dreadful yellow color. The doctor said all he needed was rest and food, but that was more than he could give him.

"Right after the war, before the Americans had a chance to get their P.W. camps set up, I was in a temporary prisoner camp at Kreuznach. It was pretty rugged. But I wasn't in that camp long. Most of those who were left there were discharged after six months. But since I had been in the S.S., they transferred me to Regensburg for two or three years."

"That was when, Franz?"

"At the end of 1945," he replied, continuing hurriedly, as if to get his story over with as soon as possible.

"The morale in those camps is wretched, Maria. At Regensburg there was always enough to eat, but it was the terrible monotony that almost drove us crazy. If you think life is monotonous here, you ought to see what it's like in a P.W. camp."

"What were your living quarters like there, Franz?" Maria asked.

"They were barracks which the Germans had used for their own prisoners. They were much the same, when it comes to comfort, as any refugee camp is inside." He smiled briefly.

"As I was saying, Maria, the worst thing about it was the lack of spirit and morale. The young fellows, having lost their faith in Nazism, were left without anything. Life had no meaning. Might made right. Sometimes I wondered myself if there was a difference between right and wrong. People didn't care what they did or said because they didn't believe in anything and didn't have any hope in God at all. It was terrible."

He ran his fingers through his hair, gazing hard at the floor.

"Then one day the most amazing thing happened. I had come in from my work on the grounds and was about to wash for supper when I met an American officer in the hall. He told me that someone had come to see me. He moved a little, and a young man stepped out from behind him. He wasn't much older than I. He grabbed my hand and talked to me in *Platt*. I couldn't believe my ears. I took him into my room, and he told me that he represented our brethren in the United States and Canada."

Franz paused for a moment, and Maria noticed that he blushed. "We talked for hours, and I guess I shed a few tears. When he left, he told me that he would pray for me and that the MCC would intercede to try to help me get an early release. Within six months, I got my papers. Naturally, I came right to Gronau."

"I guess the MCC has put in a word for several Mennonite boys in P.W. camps," Maria said to break Franz' awkward silence. She was glad the story was finished when the children pushed through the curtain, dutifully put the dishes back in their place on the end of the table, and sat down, one each side of Franz.

"Where do you live, Franz?" Rosie asked.

"Oh, I live in the bachelors' room," Franz laughed. "You know, that's up on the second floor."

"Why aren't you married, Franz?" This again from Rosie.

"Don't you think that's asking Cousin Franz a rather personal question?" Maria chuckled. She thought Hansie was unpredictable, but this from Rosie! Then she looked at Franz for his answer. After all, she had a curiosity on the subject herself.

He grinned his carefree grin that lied to the world that he had no troubles.

"Who, me? Never. I'm a woman hater, that is, except for little Rosie here."

Fortunately, Maria thought, Hansie didn't notice Rosie's sudden change of color.

"Me, too," Hansie announced firmly. "Girls, bah!"

This was too much for Rosie. "Maybe Franz is a woman hater," she declared, "but not you, Hansie. Just this afternoon I saw you and Irm—"

"Be quiet, will you?" Hansie was on his feet, pushing Rosie against the west wall. A scream on the other side of the blanket and a crash followed. Franz led them all in racing to the next room. Maria followed close on his heels, apologizing profusely to the old couple who were picking up a chair and some tin plates from the floor.

"It's all right," the old doctor laughed. "It scared Mom for a minute, but otherwise just broke the monotony of the evening."

They chatted merrily for a few more minutes, and Maria's family returned to their room.

"Really, I'd better go," Franz said, refusing the invitation to sit down again. "But don't worry, I'll be back.

You don't know how much it means to me to have a family again."

"Don't forget our hike tomorrow," Hansie called out.

"I certainly won't."

"Mother," Rosie said, when Franz had finally made his exit, "I think tomorrow I may have to tell the teacher what the verse for my motto will be. Can you tell me your idea?"

The children snuggled close to Maria as she read from the twenty-seventh Psalm,

> The Lord is my light and my salvation:
>   Whom shall I fear?
> The Lord is the strength of my life;
>   Of whom shall I be afraid?

"It is a good verse to look at often and live by," they all agreed. Then they crawled into bed, aware of the goodness of a God who not only had restored them to one another and given them a new friend but had promised them His own presence and watchful care. Of whom need they be afraid?

18

ANOTHER RAILROAD STATION, another bomb-beaten terminal. It seemed to Hans that his life would always be punctuated with *Bahnhoefen,* for he was ever on the go, pressing westward. Too long he had stayed this time. Too many wretched months he had lived in Berlin, the city with the great, shattered heart, with its endless bread queues, its desolation of ruins, its walking corpses. He didn't care where he went, but he had to get out of Berlin.

Railroad stations! How he hated them! Hated them because they reminded him of a succession of tragedies, like the day his father was deported by train to Siberia; like the night he had kissed Maria and left her crying behind while he went to face army life in the *Wehrmacht;* like that fateful trip he had made with baby Lenie, and the empty trip homeward with its agonizing end.

Lumbering casually to the ticket window, Hans bought his ticket and checked the train schedule.

"It's going to be a little late," the agent warned, then added wryly, "Maybe more than a little. Who knows? Better plan to sit down and wait a while, anyhow."

Sit down! Hans was tired of sitting. Was he an old woman, or was he a man? How his hands ached for a good, steady job! Several times while he was in Berlin he had secured temporary jobs, cleaning bricks. But most of the time he had been unemployed, walking the streets, talking to other "bums" along the way, gathering information on the one subject that obsessed him—ways and methods of crossing the border "black."

Hans was not long in finding out that it was not money that he needed to get across the border into one of the western zones. For the Reichsmark was practically worthless. In an economy where the basic necessities of life were at a premium, butter, eggs, lard, potatoes, bread, coffee, and the so-called "essential" cigarettes talked, but the voice of the mark could scarcely be heard. He needed a few marks, of course, to pay the railroad fare to his destination, but he had to have something more substantial than money to buy off people, to get the favors he needed along the way.

Once he had tried to trade his watch for a few cartons of cigarettes, thinking that he could later use the cigarettes to his advantage on the trip. But everyone to whom he offered the watch laughed in his face.

"What do we want with watches?" one black marketeer had asked him when he tried to make the deal. "That is a luxury, man. We want food."

And so, in desperation, he had left Berlin for a short time, hiring himself out to a farmer. The farmer soon saw that he had had a rural background and was glad for his help during the early harvesting. When he could no longer use Hans, he gladly paid him in kind. And how rich Hans had felt as he lugged the heavy sack of potatoes he had earned back to Berlin! Not for a moment would he let those potatoes out of his sight; by night they were his pillow, by day his constant companion.

Hans dropped into an empty seat, assumed his usual slouch, and watched the milling crowd around him. A neatly dressed woman, probably wearing her best clothes, reached into her handbag and brought out a black bun. Hans was hungry himself, but he did not dare spend any money on food if he really wanted to leave Berlin. A mother, dragging five little children around and behind her, entered the door. Her hands were busy with the young ones, but her eyes darted like searchlights to and fro. Her face was haggard. She reminded Hans of the woman who lived in a bunker down the street from him, a sick widow who with her children simply existed in a room where there was no light, no bedding, and almost no food. More than once he had caught sight of the children scavenging for garbage or dashing helter-skelter on the streets in search of kindling.

Indeed, postwar Berlin, with its population of over 3,000,000, its slender threads of transportation, its miles of rubble, had been a depressing place in which to live. Physically, it was crushed; politically, it was divided between four great nations and situated in the middle of Russian-occupied territory. The atmosphere was tense, the people dejected. Hans often felt like a small boy, lost from his mother, wandering about homeless, unemployed, unwanted, and *alone*.

Restless, he meandered slowly out of doors again. He dared not go far, but he hated sitting in that smoky station. Better to stand on the street and watch the passing crowd, tiresome as that might become, than to sit idly with hands folded in that stuffy, churning depot.

"Oh, I'm sorry."

He did not see the withered old lady until he had knocked one of the heavy sacks from her arms. Hastily he picked up the bag of sticks, careful to save each tiny twig that tumbled from the opening. Then he found himself staring at her face, thinking that she must be at least seventy years old, that she could be his own mother. The twigs were too heavy for her; they weighed her down unbearably.

"Thank you," she smiled at him. "Not everyone is so kind to an old woman."

The assurance that he was glad to help her gave her courage to ask another favor.

"Can you tell me, sir, how I can get to Brenzstrasse from here?" She laid her sacks down, sitting on one of them and panting wearily.

"It is not far, four blocks left, then three blocks right."

Suddenly Hans felt an impulsive wave of sympathy for the motherly old soul. "Are you alone?" He almost added, "too."

"No, I lost all my children, but Papa and I still have each other." Her eyes filled with tears. "We can't go out together, because we have only one pair of shoes between the two of us. It's my turn to wear them today, and Papa's turn to rest."

And when he had helped to load her sacks on her back, she was gone, leaving him angry again, angry at the God Maria believed in, a God who allowed things like that to happen.

Hans knew that he was stubborn, that he had his faults, but one thing they could not say about him: he was not unmindful of the heartbreaks of others. Proud skeptic that he was, he was at the same time so softhearted that other people's troubles automatically became his own. Maybe that was why he was disappointed in a God who remained aloof to man's predicament, who didn't do something about people like that poor old woman. Hans was only a man, but if he had in his hands the power they gave this God credit for, he knew he would do a better job of ruling the universe.

Of course, the train was late. Because of the fuel shortage, trains in postwar Germany were few and crowded; as a result of the disruption in service caused by the war, station stops were long and confused. Hour closed in upon hour while Hans stood, leaning against the outer wall of the *Bahnhof,* standing birdlike on one foot and then the other, vowing over and over to himself that this would be his last hour in Berlin. Soon he would taste freedom, *freedom,* FREEDOM!

But while he waited he watched humanity hobble by, a wasted people with weary feet, weakened bodies, and warped spirits. Ideals and idealism lay shattered at the feet of the typical Berliner, for people today did not go around thinking beautiful, glorious thoughts. Elemental demands of life—a bucket of coal, a half pound of coffee, a couple of cigarettes, a loaf of bread, or an item of clothing—were the main concerns, and no one cared how he got these things.

And, after all, if there was a God, would He blame a man for "organizing" a few stolen potatoes for a hungry family? Would He condemn a mother, who, tired of the endless search for food, the penetrating cold, the ever-gnawing hunger pains, finally decided to end it all for her children and herself?

Hans had shuffled from the inside of the station to the street and back again many times, in order to stay clear of the excited mob who thronged the building. When, however, an unmistakably clear whistle announced from the distance that a train was approaching, Hans darted for the platform, plunging through the crowd with a determination and lack of courtesy that he had learned during the past months.

Getting on the train was strictly a matter of survival of the fittest. Thousands waited as the train pulled up. Feelings ran high, old ladies begged not to be crushed to death, shouts and curses filled the air. Crowded into an eight-person compartment with twenty-nine fellow passengers, Hans felt that he was buried alive. Outside, people screamed, sobbed, and moaned as the train shoved forward. Inside, everyone sighed with relief. For they were aboard the train, were headed for their destinations, and were lucky that they did not have to hang on the outside as many other passengers were compelled to do.

In order to camouflage his reason for entering the suspicion-laden radius of the border itself, Hans chose to break his trip halfway between Berlin and the Russian-American zonal division. The train, a slow local, stopped at almost every station to let passengers off, city people who were out to buy a few chickens or potatoes from farmer friends or relatives. At every stop it seemed the train would never move again. Thus, it was midnight, four hours after Hans left Berlin, when he finally got off the train. There was no official check on the passengers during this first leg of his journey.

Hans had talked for hours with people who had received letters from friends in the American and British zones, acquaintances who had made it successfully across the border "black." He had planned his course of action well. Yet he was nervous about his venture into the unknown. Indeed, he had been told that only about 40 per cent of those refugees who attempted this feat arrived safely on the other side. One only needed to make one error of judgment, one slip of the tongue, one misstep along the way, to fall into a self-made grave along the road.

For the border line that divided the east and west zones was well fortified with towers from which East Zone soldiers could see for many kilometers. Moreover, soldiers on foot and trained watchdogs were ever on the alert for men, women, and children who were trying to sneak across to the other side. There was a legal way to cross the border, but there were few who had the proper papers to cross the "Red Sea" legitimately. The best solution was to find a man of confidence who had lived in the area all his life, who knew the paths to take, and who would, for a given fee, escort the traveler to safety. Hans had not been able to get the name of a specific man because of the necessary secrecy, but he knew that there were such men to be found. He was determined to take the risk.

19

It was on the second train, early the next morning, that Hans got his first clue. They were no longer close to any large city, and the compartment was not crowded. Hans even had a seat. Ever cautious about strangers, he ignored his seatmate, staring, bored and fidgety, through the dusty window.

His neighbor, however, soon proved himself to be the sociable type. So long as he did the talking, Hans accommodated him with an occasional nod or smile of agreement. He was a thin young fellow with keen eyes and a know-it-all smirk.

As they neared their destination, the inevitable happened. Making a routine stop, the train was suddenly boarded by East Zone soldiers, checking on passengers' tickets and their reasons for traveling into the guarded zone. Hans pulled his ticket from his pocket, set his face as nonchalantly as he could, and reviewed the story in his mind, as he had been trying to do all the way from Hengstfeld.

"You, fellow!" the officer shouted to Hans. Hans' partner had just explained that he was returning to Rager from a necessary business trip to Berlin. Rager was his home town, and he had papers to prove it.

"You! Where are *your* papers?"

"I have none along, sir, but my residence is Hengstfeld and I am visiting my old uncle at his request."

The soldier lifted his eyebrows.

"And what, may I ask, is this uncle's name?"

"Arthur Baumann." So confidently did Hans answer that he would almost have believed his story himself.

But the soldier was not yet satisfied.

"What's his address in Rager?"

"Two thirty-two Hauptstrasse." There was a "Main Street" in every town. That, too, Hans had carefully thought through.

The soldier's face registered a question mark. Just then another officer interrupted him. "I'll be back," he said, joining the other inspector in a loud argument with a passenger in the next coach.

Hans held his breath, but the soldier did not return for what must have been ten minutes, and when he did come back he proceeded to the seat in front of Hans.

"Pretty good liar, aren't you?" Hans' chuckling seatmate chided, when the soldiers were out of earshot.

"What do you mean?" Hans demanded, resentful that the youngster could see through him so easily.

"Oh, nothing at all, except that I saw you get on the other train in Berlin."

Hans reddened. "You must be mistaken."

The mouth widened into another grin.

"Another thing, I happen to live on Hauptstrasse in Rager. There's no 232. I live at the end of the street, and my number is 105."

The station in Rager came into view in the distance, and the heckler moved to get up.

"But never mind," he went on, seeing that Hans was taken aback. "Don't let it worry you."

He lowered his voice.

"If you need a name to help you across, I know a

man who really knows the country. He's helped a lot of my friends. What'll you give me if I give you his card? I don't know what you've got in your sack, but I might be able to strike a bargain."

Hans thought fast. Was this young fellow telling the truth, or might he be taking advantage of him? Who knew but that he might even be a spy! He hesitated.

"Look, brother, I'm not fooling you. I'm being square about it. I told you my address. There's no catch to it."

"All right. You give me the card, and I'll slip two kilo of potatoes into your sack. That's all I can spare. Is that all right?"

"It's a deal."

The stranger watched Hans count out the potatoes, judging the weight from his own long experience in this type of bartering. The potatoes were large ones and both were satisfied that they weighed about two kilo. Then he gave Hans the proffered card and watched him scan its contents.

"Well, good luck, friend, you'll need it."

And he was gone, leaving Hans stupefied at the apparent luck that had come his way. *I guess,* he thought, smiling to himself, *Maria would call this an answer to prayer!*

20

UNCERTAINTY, however, clouded Hans' every thought as he got off the train in Rager. He had been lucky, so far, but the worst of his venture was yet to come. What was more, the questioning of the soldiers and the prying of the officious seatmate had left him a bit shaky.

Depositing the precious name card in his inside pocket, Hans strode quickly through the small station and out into the fresh air. It was important that he walk confidently, that he look as though he were going some place. Loitering aimlessly around might throw suspicion upon him; he couldn't be sure that he would not meet those soldiers again.

Rager apparently was small enough that it had been left intact during the war. It was not unlike any other little German city which he had seen: narrow cobblestone streets, an occasional church spire pointing skyward above the chimneys, humble little houses closely lining the streets with windows thrown open and bedding hanging out to air. Pale-faced children played dreamily in the streets; old men sat and watched their world pass by; young mothers hustled downtown to stand in bread lines or to the country to bargain and barter enough to feed their nestlings at home.

Adjusting his potato sack on his back, Hans limbered his stiff muscles in a quick walk down Bahnhofstrasse. The name on the card in his pocket indicated a shoe repair shop on Moerickestrasse. Probably the kind of a deal, Hans thought, that one would make in broad daylight under the pretense of ordinary business.

He paused long enough to examine his own shoes. Surely they were authentically in need of repair! He did not cherish memories of the past winter in Berlin, standing around on icy streets with frost-bitten toes. Only one fear haunted him as he sought out the little shop. Could he trust that stranger on the train? How could he be sure that this was not a diabolical trick? There were people low enough to play a game with human hearts and souls as forfeits.

Hans took his time in looking the town over, getting a good idea of the lay of the land, until he was sure that shops would be open. Thus it was midmorning of a sultry day when he set out for Moerickestrasse. Mopping beads of perspiration from his forehead, he was glad that Rager was not large and that the shop was not situated in the cluttered business section of town. Instead, Moerickestrasse took him through a quiet park. Beneath spreading elms he found the shingle, "Reynold Bresher, Shoe Repair."

An enterprising shoe repairman, to be sure, he mused, resuming a casual nonchalance and slowing his gait to the heat of the day.

"Herr Bresher?" he asked, hoping against hope that the man he sought was not this young apprentice who met him when he entered.

"To the back of the shop, sir," the boy motioned, picking up his tool again and whistling as he resumed his work.

Hans picked his way through the disorganized equipment and blinked in the semidarkness of the back room.

When his eyes became accustomed to the dark, he saw a short, middle-aged man, sturdily built, shrewd in his glance. He waited patiently while Bresher finished an explanation about a shoe he had fixed.

"Sorry, but all we could do was to patch it. Did as neat a job as you could get anywhere. Should be good for another six months."

The customer shrugged his stooped shoulders and frowned. "If it's the best you can do, it will have to do, but six months from now I'll probably be going barefoot."

Bresher pretended not to hear the other man's dissatisfied grunts, abruptly turning to Hans with a "what-can-I-do-for-you?" expression.

"My shoes," Hans said quickly, noting that the other customer was not yet out of earshot. "I know they are very bad, but they will have to do me for considerable time. How much would you charge to fix them up?"

The other customer departed and Hans took his shoe off for closer inspection.

"————! You fellows bring me shoes that are ready for the dump and then get excited if I can't make them look like new. I'll see what I can do, but you'll have to be satisfied with the results."

He shifted his attention from the shoe to Hans' face. "I prefer payment in kind. Got any cigarettes?"

Hans breathed deep. He would get it over with before any other people came into the shop. "I've got a nice sack of big potatoes here," he said, motioning toward the bundle at his feet. "I do want my shoes repaired, but someone gave me your card on the train as I came into Rager. I would also like—"

He deliberated, watching the other man cautiously.

Bresher dropped the piece of leather in his hand. "May I see the card?" he muttered under his breath, glancing about to be sure no one was around.

Then he clasped his hands together.

"Yes, yes, yes! I'm the man who can help you." He came closer to be sure his whispers would not be overheard.

"Tonight?"

"As soon as possible, sir."

"How many potatoes can you give?"

"You can have all of them."

"Fine. You can leave them here right now. There won't be time to pay tonight. Know this town?"

"Walked all over it this morning."

"I'll make the directions simple. Go down Bahnhofstrasse past the depot for five blocks. Here's a pencil—better write it down. Turn off on Panoramaweg and follow that street for one kilometer. Got it? Residential section. Meet you at the clump of trees on right side of Panoramaweg. Nine o'clock. Yes?"

"Yes!"

Bresher leaned over a worktable and gazed hard at Hans.

"Have you the directions clearly in mind?"

"I'm sure I do."

"Then we'll meet tonight."

He shook Hans' hand with finality and suddenly brushed past him to meet a new customer. Hans knew from the way in which he was dismissed that his shoe repair was forgotten. But he didn't care. He would not have even thought of having them repaired, had he not needed an excuse to meet Bresher.

The day passed slowly. Hans had a lot of time to think, far too much time, though he was accustomed to idleness. He retraced his steps to the picturesque little park and ate his day's supply of bread there. Finally, bored by an old man in the park who wanted to talk, he took new routes through the town, locating Panoramaweg and browsing through a newspaper in a little bookstore.

Anything to pass the time! Hans tried hard to cover his inward anxiety with an outward composure. He even tried to force himself to think of other things, but like a boomerang his thoughts always returned to the night's adventure. Was Bresher to be trusted? Would he really be at Panoramaweg, now that he had Hans' potatoes?

But the hour arrived at last. Hans was not late for his eerie appointment. And Bresher was there! The older man gave Hans a quick, penetrating look that made him feel naive and self-conscious.

"Do you swim?"

"Not very well."

"Hmmm. Then that's out." Bresher leaned against a tree, staring abstractedly at his heavy dusty boots.

"I know two good routes. I think they're both still safe. One is farther away from the watchtower than the other. Have to be a fairly good swimmer or you wouldn't make it. Stream separates the two zones in that spot. Other way you'll have to wade through marshes. Plenty of dodging. Willing to take the risk?"

Hans nodded soberly. He had little to lose.

The guide pulled his shoestrings hard. "Then we'd

better get started. It's a good night. The guards won't be able to see far because of the fog."

He paused impressively.

"But they'll be more vigilant; so we'll have to be careful."

"Will you go the whole way with me?" Hans queried, as they walked toward the edge of town. He thought after he had asked it that he had sounded like Hansie wanting his father's protection.

"You cooperate and don't get me in trouble, and I'll take you most of the way. You'll be able to make it the rest of the way by yourself."

Hans wished that he had not asked it. It sounded silly and cowardly. Must be getting soft, he thought to himself, remembering the rough months he had spent in the *Wehrmacht*. There were months of rigid discipline, days of dodging bullets that whistled over and around and above his head, nights of weary numbness in foxholes, long hours with little food, mountain-sized minutes packed with fear and horror.

Suddenly the dreadful quietness of the night was broken by the sound of two shots, not very far away.

"Say, fellow, get hold of yourself. You're downright jumpy."

"Sorry."

"It won't happen to you. I can guarantee that. Probably some fool who tried it alone. And the shots may have missed."

But they probably didn't. Hans knew that much himself. He squinted and tried to peer ahead, in the direction of the shots.

"They didn't seem to come from the tower, did they?"

he wondered aloud, padding along behind his guide through an open field. He judged that he and Bresher were about a kilometer from the tower.

"Watch your step here," the man advised, ignoring his question. "It's pretty slushy. Keep out of the mud. Stay close."

Stopping frequently to stare into the darkness and listen, the two men came to a crude shed behind a little farmhouse. Hans noticed a light in one room of the house peeping out from beneath well-drawn shades. Bresher strode uninhibited through the front lawn, however, paying no attention to the signs of life, pausing only on the sheltered side of the shed.

"Old couple live here," he explained casually, as though he had read Hans' mind. "Harmless as cats. I used to play here when I was a boy."

Then he crouched warily beside the shed, surveying closely the field in front of him. When he spoke, he whispered, and his breath was warm on the back of Hans' neck.

"Do you see those woods across this wheat field? When the tower lights are pointed the other way, we run. Understand?"

Again his sharp eyes inspected Hans. "Run like a deer, see? Light-footed but swift. No noises. If you sneeze, I'll break your neck. All right, go!"

Hans could run fast, even under ordinary circumstances. But never would he have believed that he could tear across a field as rapidly and yet as stealthily as he did that night. When his heavier guide made an unscheduled stop in front of him, he plunged into a bush to keep from falling over him.

Bresher was horrified. "What in ——— is the matter with you?" he swore. "A couple of noises like that and we'll both be dead."

As they pushed their way through the small patch of forest, climbing here over a stump, dodging there a hanging limb, Hans' admiration for his guide increased. Bresher himself seemed to get untold satisfaction from his own prowess, his knowledge of the countryside, his skill in pathfinding, his confidence and audacity in forging his way through a maze of hazardous holes and caches. At last they were out of the forest and in the tall, wet grasses of the marshlands.

Suddenly Hans felt security slip way beneath his feet. Bresher jerked to a standstill, and there was no doubt that he was again alarmed. Without a word, he dropped to the ground, lying flat on his face, his body camouflaged by the waving grasses. Petrified with fear, Hans did the same, but not before he saw the reason for Bresher's fright.

Not ten rods away Hans saw flashlights, not one, but two. Flashlights, husky voices, heavy tramping through the marshlands. The footsteps came closer. And closer. So close that Hans thought the officers would surely stumble over their bodies. And then they went by.

He wanted to look, after he knew they were far enough that they could no longer hear his movements. But, following Bresher's example, he lay perfectly still, careful not to stir even after they seemed many rods away. Finally, the guide pulled himself to his feet, peered around, and stretched.

"That was a close call. Closer than I've had in a long time. We're not out of danger yet. They have flashlights, and they're armed. It's not too late yet to get your brains shot out."

Then he moved a few more feet and surveyed the situation in every direction, listening and scanning the marshlands like a hunted animal.

"Duck back into the grass," he whispered, dropping on his knees. "There comes that light from the tower again. I think we'd better crawl the rest of the way. It isn't too far. It's safer."

"On our hands and knees?"

"You heard me!"

So they crawled baby-wise, wiggled worm-wise, and occasionally gained welcome relief by running for shorter stretches.

Then, all of a sudden, it was over. Bresher halted once more, pointing his finger to a few dim lights across the field from where they stood.

"All right, partner, you've made it. You've earned your freedom. Take my advice and run until you're across this field and into that town over there. Yes, and if I were you, I wouldn't stop until I'd get to Kassel."

Then he was gone, and Hans was too busy taking his advice to notice which direction he went. It was almost dawn when Hans arrived in Kassel, more bedraggled than he had ever been in his life. Beneath the mixture of blood and mud that coated him, his flesh was bruised and itchy. Every joint twinged with pain; his knees were open sores peeping from the holes in his trousers; his whole body smarted from falls he had had and obstacles he had failed to dodge.

Yet he had nothing to complain about. For he breathed the cool, clear air of freedom. And not everyone was so

163

lucky. People like that poor fellow he had stumbled over soon after Bresher had left him, freshly murdered by the very men from whom he and Bresher had hidden.

Suddenly Hans felt like offering a prayer. But to whom could he pray? He couldn't thank a God in whom he did not believe. In confusion he dropped in the grass beside the road, rolled over, and went to sleep.

21

MARIA STRAIGHTENED HER SHOULDERS and stood up to stretch her tired body. There was no use sewing longer; it was getting too dark. Almost lovingly she laid out the work of her hands on the cot, running her fingers proudly and efficiently over the dress that Rosie would wear on Sunday, the one Rosie had been dreaming about ever since the MCC worker had given Maria the two old ones.

"This is a pretty good dress, but it seems a little too short for Rosie," Maria had been told when it was her turn to receive some new clothing. "But we've got an old dress here we don't know quite what to do with. Do you think between the two you could work up a dress for your little girl?"

The two pieces of material went well together, Maria felt, and she immediately envisioned how she could sew in strips of the darker material around the bottom and waist of the dress that almost fit Rosie. Maria had fixed clothes for her daughter that had required much more ingenuity than that to make them presentable. And the other good parts of the worn dress would patch a shirt for Hansie. Gratefully Maria had returned to her room with the dresses; happily she had sewed all day to have Rosie's dress ready for a fitting that night.

She had not worked alone. Weary of her own company she had joined the seamstresses on the porch, exchanged ideas with them on renovating clothing to the best advantage, and chatted gaily throughout the afternoon. Frau Krahn was turning a suit inside out for her son, making it over completely.

"He's had to look ragged for so long," she had murmured, her scissors rapidly snipping the threads. "I'd do anything to make him look presentable at church on Sunday."

"I think a child can almost lose his self-respect if he looks under par for too long," Frau Isaak had agreed, pausing long enough to count stitches on the blouse she was knitting from wool she had received from Canada.

Irmgart's mother had laughed from the other corner of the table. "Now what would happen to Irmgart's self-respect if she had to wear this on the outside?"

Everyone had joined in her merriment as they inspected the pitiful-looking slip she held up. Susie Dyck had patched her daughter's slip so often that what was left of the original garment could scarcely be detected. But it was still a slip, and Irmgart would have to wear it until it fell apart.

Yes, it had been a pleasant afternoon, and Maria was eager to see Rosie in the dress she had almost finished. Folding the precious garment, she laid it away, wondering why the children didn't come home from school. She wished she could live before them the words which Rosie had so carefully printed on their wall motto. But it seemed that with the loss of Lenie and Hans, she found herself clinging harder to the children, worrying about them more than she should. Sometimes she struggled long and hard before she could add "Thy will be done" to her prayers.

There was a soft flapping of the entrance curtain and Maria heard a man's voice just outside her room.

"Mailman!" Franz' quizzical face peeped cautiously around the curtain. "I stopped over at the office on my way home and they asked me to bring you this. Guess people are getting used to the fact that we're all in the same family."

Again he gave her one of those kinship grins that were his specialty.

"Thanks, Franz. But who would be writing to me?" Her eyes scanned the foreign stamp, the neatly inscribed return address. "It couldn't be—no, it couldn't be—"

She sat down on the cot, her fingers trembly as she ripped open the letter.

"Franz, Franz," she exclaimed, when she had looked at the signature and read the first paragraph, "Tante Erika is still alive in Canada! She emigrated from Chortitza in 1926, but we haven't heard from her since the war. You wouldn't remember her, of course, but she is your great-aunt and my aunt. We didn't see much of her in Russia because she lived quite a distance from our village. But now she has checked with the MCC to see if any of her relatives are still living. And they told her about us."

Her eyes scanned the contents of the letter, then she looked again at the address on the envelope.

From Tante Erika, dear old Tante Erika. But she was not so old when she left Chortitza; she still had half-grown children. Ni-a-gar-a, On-tar-i-o, Canada."

So many people in camp boasted of letters from relatives in America, that Maria had more than once checked her own inner impulse to covet a letter for herself. She had more than once wondered if any of Tante Erika's family were still living. She had more than once hushed the children's wistful remarks that they wished someone would send *them* a package from Canada. Even in her fondest dreams she had scarcely hoped for a letter, for she long ago had lost Tante Erika's address.

"Well, I'll let you alone with your letter. I ought to be going anyway." Franz turned his cap over in his hand and headed for the doorway.

"No, no, please stay, Franz. Wait and see what more Tante Erika has to say. I want to share my happiness."

Maria noticed that he sat down gladly, leaning back and relaxing on the cot as though her room were home. She knew that he had only been pretending busyness, that he was bored every time he had to leave for his dingy corner of the bachelors' quarters.

The letter was written in simple handwriting, but was a little difficult to read because Tante Erika was old and her fingers shaky. It went on to tell that all of her children were now married: Jacob was bookkeeper in a lumber company; Helmut was employed in a dairy; Kate had married a prosperous farmer and had three children of her own. She, Tante Erika, lived comfortably in an apartment in Kate's spacious farmhouse. Maria read aloud, commenting to Franz between lines, rejoicing at the good fortune of her aunt.

"The Mennonite Central Committee has written to me, in answer to my inquiry, that you, dear Maria, and your two children are right there in camp. Kate and her husband for a long time have had the conviction that they should help someone to come to this country, someone of our own brothers and sisters who are stranded in Europe. John is also very much in need of help here on the farm. We had not dared to hope that we would find someone so closely related to us. Would you want to emigrate to Canada, to come and live with us here in Ontario, to bring your children and rear them here?"

"Franz!" Maria sighed. "Do you realize what this letter means? Canada—I did not dare dream of such a thing."

Then her smile faded.

"But it is impossible, of course, so long as we don't know where Hans is. If we knew he were in Siberia, it would be different. But I refuse to believe that he is. If he would come soon, then we could all go together! Oh, Franz, wouldn't that be wonderful?"

She looked at the youthful face studying hers from across the table.

"Perhaps you, too, Franz, could go to Canada. Shall I write to her that you are here? Would you want to go to Canada as a close relative?"

Maria had never seen Franz look as he did then, almost as though he could break down and cry.

"I'm afraid, Maria, that Canada may not have me."

She looked at him, distressed.

"Why, Franz? There's nothing wrong with you physically, is there?"

"It's what I mentioned to you before. They turned down two others from the bachelors' ward in the last few days. One of these days I'll be examined by the International Refugee Organization and the Canadian officials and they'll question me up and down. I have no proof at all that I was forced into the German Army, even into the Secret Service. It was the same with the other two boys. They were rejected politically."

169

He brushed some mud from the cuff of his pants. Maria felt a mother's pity for him. Why did happiness always have to be mixed with sorrow? If Franz could not go to Canada, her own joy seemed illegitimate.

And then, it was as if a thunderbolt struck her—Hans, too, had been in the *Wehrmacht*. Suppose—suppose she went to Canada and he came through to Gronau, only to find that he could not follow her!

Franz sensed the cloud he had thrown over Maria's burst of sunlight. He felt inexpressibly sorry.

"Oh, come, Cousin Maria, let's cheer up and go over to the immigration office and see what the MCC has to say about your letter. It's too good to sit around brooding over."

That's the way Franz was. The experiences he had been through, even his uncertain future, never spoiled his joy in living for long. If life did not furnish him entertainment, he got busy and manufactured some small pleasure, whittling a toy for a child, swapping stories with someone in the camp, or strumming absent-mindedly on his guitar. Quickly he tossed his own troubles to the winds, taking Maria by the arm and leading her somewhat hesitant body toward the MCC office.

"It's beautiful outside right now, isn't it?" Maria remarked, her soul breathing in the beauty of the tree-lined street. "Changing the subject, Franz, what should I say when I get over there? Shall I take this as God's leading, or shall I wait for Hans? I haven't lost hope—I just can't—but I have no proof that he isn't in Siberia looking for us."

"Just tell them about your letter and ask their advice."

"But—oh, say, there's Frieda. She's one of the stenographers in the office—" Maria waved at the figure crossing the street toward her. "Elfrieda, you're just the person we want to see."

Elfrieda looked extra pretty today, Maria thought. How much better she appeared now that she had put on a little weight at the camp. Her hair was braided becomingly around her head; her clothes were spotless. And that smile!

"Maria, I'm ashamed that I haven't been over to see you since you're out of the hospital. Honestly, we've been working so hard in the office. We've been at it until midnight every night this week. But it's *so* satisfying, knowing that another transport will be sailing next week for Paraguay."

"It must be. I envy your feeling of accomplishment, Frieda. Oh, excuse me, surely you have met my cousin, Franz? I just took for granted that you knew each other."

Maria was aware, all of a sudden, that Franz was ill at ease, shifting uneasily from foot to foot, quickly looking away from Elfrieda when she caught him gazing steadily at the girl.

"Of course we know each other," Elfrieda replied. "We sing in the choir together."

"You mean you sing in the choir," he laughed. "I'm there bodily, but I'm afraid I'm not good for much more than moral support."

Again he stared at Elfrieda so steadily that she blushed. Maria came to the rescue.

"Frieda, I just received a letter inviting me to emigrate to my cousin's farm in Canada. Should I show it to the MCC?"

Elfrieda beamed. Explaining that Maria should take

171

the letter to Herr Peters, the refugee office manager whom everyone knew and loved, she hurried on to the camp and Franz, too, left to make his way uptown on some business of his own.

Maria crossed the street toward the villa, the letter a firm and material proof that she was not dreaming. Her heart fluttered anxiously; a new hope swelled within her breast. Suppose that she could take the children to a new home, that they could grow up to adulthood in a normal way, that they could look forward to a future free from fear, far away from this continent of woe? Suppose that Rosie would marry comfortably and settle on a farm and have three children, and Hansie—

The sight of Herr Peters leaning over a desk, the sound of four typewriters clicking at once, the low murmur of stenographers consulting together over a letter, brought Maria out of her dream world. Slowly she found her voice, laying the letter on the desk beneath Herr Peters' kind face.

"It's from relatives in Canada. They want us to live with them."

Her voice echoed back in her own ears, and what she had said sent a strange quivering through her body.

They *want* us—they *want* us— someone *wants* a homeless, unwanted refugee. They *want* us—

22

THE BALMY MAY DAY was perfect, just right to warm up the spirits and bones of those who were lucky enough to be outside, a wonderful day to be perched on a chair, under a tree, peeling potatoes. At least, that seemed to be the opinion of the group of women who sat in a circle around a big tub of water, tossing in potatoes as they laughed and chattered together.

Maria was glad to be busy again, thrilled to be making a contribution, however small, to the community life about her. The doctor had finally given her permission to work, and the *Lagerleiter* had assigned her an easy job to start on. For the past few weeks since her release from the hospital Maria had watched with interest this most unusual community in which she lived. It was a community born not merely out of social and economic needs, not simply because the inhabitants liked living together because of their common religious heritage, but as a result of love—the love of friends and relatives in another land.

She had felt the heartbeat of this strange community; she had observed the efficient way in which the camp administration channeled the variety of abilities into the multiple jobs that it took to run the camp smoothly. Cleaning squads worked incessantly. In the basement washwomen bent and perspired over old-time washboards and hand-turned wooden machines. Conscientiously performing their duties in the newly converted MCC hospital, nurses dressed in blue uniforms hurried from room to room. In a small, poorly equipped shop two shoemakers did the best they could, and in a similarly primitive shop two young boys and two older men repaired chairs and other furniture. On the veranda seamstresses visited while they repaired and remodeled clothing. Cooks in the kitchen were ever busy preparing the three meals a day that kept this huge community alive and active. In the camp office, workers admitted new people, grappled with problems concerning the physical operation of the camp, distributed rations and supplies according to the needs of the individual campers, assigned workers to their specific tasks. Workers in the MCC office labored far into the night to prepare documents and letters to make possible the migration of a continual stream of displaced persons to Canada, the United States, and Paraguay.

And now, after a few weeks in which Maria had become stronger, the doctor had at last said that she might do some light work. Help was desperately needed, for a large influx of refugees from other parts of the British and American zones had come in to be transported to Bremerhaven, where they were to sail for Paraguay on the *S.S. Charleton Monarch.* Since the camp, which usually accommodated a maximum of 900 persons, was filled to capacity, these approximately 1,000 guests slept *en masse* on straw-covered floors in school buildings which had been released by the city for that purpose. Of course, these newcomers had to be fed as well, and the kitchen force had to be doubled to take care of the emergency.

Maria looked down at her apron-covered lap and her

own busy fingers with satisfaction. New life surged within her; the fresh air of spring filled her lungs. Deftly her knife slipped around the potato in her hand. So content she felt within herself that she almost forgot the circle of friends around her.

A sudden shuffling of feet and hustling of young bodies terminated the numerous conversations around the potato pile, as everyone turned to watch the school children form queues in front of the *Klubhaus*. Maria's eyes met Susie Dyck's and they both smiled. Their children were whispering together as they marched toward the school building. Hansie's friendship with pretty little Irmgart was firmly established, despite the teasing of his boy friends and the insinuating remarks of his young sister.

"There goes the Guenther child," Frau Duerksen said, pointing out a thin little form at the end of the line. "They were at it again last night, and this morning it was terrible."

"You'd think that anybody lucky enough to have their whole family with them could get along." Frau Enns' tone was severe as she tossed another potato into the tub. Maria saw bitterness sketched in hard lines upon the woman's face. Frau Enns had not been mellowed by the loss of her husband and both of her children; her deep-rooted resentment of life many times sprang forth in sharp words of criticism, or in angry, sarcastic remarks.

Maria hated gossip. She wanted to turn the tide of the conversation, but her nerve failed her. She was too new among the women to wield much influence.

And what was more, Frau Duerksen wanted to finish what she had started. The carpenter's fights with his wife were always excellent material for gossip.

175

"They surely don't try to keep their voices down when they quarrel. I guess half of the people in the Klubhaus heard her tell him off this morning."

What was the use of rehashing something that too many people had already heard? Unfortunately, the thin blanket walls were anything but soundproof. Family difficulties that might have been easily cleared up were almost impossible to mend after they had been shared by so many outsiders. Maria tried to swallow the feeling of disgust that flared up within her. She looked help-lessly at Irmgart's mother. It was easy to see that she, too, was annoyed.

Maria had not learned to know Frau Dyck as well as her son had become acquainted with Irmgart, but she had noticed that Susie Dyck was an interesting, spirited person, one who never allowed her lonely widowed life to sink down too far in the mire of despondency.

Susie Dyck threw a naked potato into the kettle and stood up to stretch herself. Everybody looked up in surprise at her snappy change of conversation.

"My, I'm really achy in the bones this morning," she said. "Wonder what the people feel like who had to sleep on the floor of the school building last night?"

"Especially the older people," Frau Neufeld added.

Frau Enns' face lost its sharp look and her eyes filled with tears. "I'll never forget trying to keep my dad alive on the flight into Germany." She paused, forgetting the work of her hands, then added painfully, "He died on the way, he and my only little son."

It was Susie Dyck who rescued the conversation once more. Get started on a theme like that, and they would all be weeping into the potato kettle. And not for Frau

Enns, but for their own griefs, their own private and multiplied heartbreaks. Maria for her Hans and her Lenie, her mother and father and aunts and uncles; Frau Duerksen for her son lost in battle, for her husband transported to Siberia, for her mother lost along the trek; Susie Dyck for Irmgart's little brother who died of starvation on the flight from Russia into Poland; Frau Neufeld for her parents who were murdered before her eyes.

"The worst thing about it," Susie Dyck continued, "is that these poor people have been here so long, and every time they think that the *Charleton Monarch* will sail, the MCC gets word from the officials that it has to be postponed again."

"And the outbreak of measles in the camp doesn't help anything," Frau Wiebe informed from her corner. "I ought to know. My daughter works over in the office, and I guess they really have a mix-up. They get one family processed for Paraguay and they all pass the physical and everything, and then one child in their family gets the measles before the ship leaves and they have to put somebody else in their place."

Maria recalled what Elfrieda had told her just the night before, when she had met her on the way back from the office, heavy-eyed from long hours of hard work.

"If there were only a good isolation ward available, maybe the MCC could check the epidemic," Frau Wiebe continued. "My daughter Margaretha just remarked last night that the camp doctor is almost frantic trying to find enough rooms to isolate the children who have measles."

She stopped, as if suddenly remembering something.

"Oh, maybe I'm talking out of turn. Margaretha warned me not to repeat things from the office."

Nobody liked Frau Wiebe, for she always had advance information on things, doling it out with miserly care and overbearing superiority. But each one listened eagerly when these morsels were cast forth, hoping to learn something that would throw light on her own "case."

In spite of Frau Wiebe's pang of conscience, she would have transmitted a little more of her knowledge had not Herr Peters appeared at that moment from the veranda door.

"Herr Peters, Herr Peters, could you come here for a moment?" Susie Dyck's eyes sparkled mischievously. Maria looked admiringly at Susie's slim figure and entertained two thoughts simultaneously. Susie was acting on an impulse and Irmgart surely did look like her mother.

Herr Peters obliged, and stood looking down on the little circle of women from his advantageous height with a pleasing mixture of responsible dignity and fatherly affection. He was built over a large strong frame, and there was strength of character and personality about him that made him a natural leader.

"And what can I do for you?"

Susie beamed, enjoying the opportunity of getting more up-to-date information than the usually informed Frau Wiebe.

"Is the *Charleton Monarch* really going to sail next Wednesday?"

Herr Peters burst out in a guffaw, and when he laughed, he laughed all over his face. It was a wholesome sight.

"If that isn't like a woman to ask a question that only

the Lord and the International Refugee Organization know the answer to. My dear lady, if you find out the answer, be sure to let us know."

All eyes rested on Susie, but she was nothing abashed. Herr Peters' fun-making was not meant to be cruel. His sense of humor, like his faith in God, was a saving element in many a serious situation that confronted the office force.

"I'm glad *I'm* going to Canada," she grinned up at him. "While you're not answering questions, when is my sailing date?"

"Oh, next year sometime, if you're good."

"Say, Herr Peters," Frau Neufeld popped up from her quiet observation in the corner, "I just got a letter yesterday from my nephew who went to Canada, and what do you think? He's just been there six months and he already has a car!"

"A car! In six months!" Everyone gasped. Automobiles in Europe were owned only by a wealthy few.

Frau Enns, however, showed no surprise. Gravely she nodded her head. "Oh, sure. They have everything in Canada and the United States. Over here only a few are wealthy; over there only a few are poor."

Herr Peters' smile became a frown.

"Now look, I have to get back to the office, but before I go I want every one of you to listen. That is a mistaken idea that too many of our people have. Our brethren in America have been blessed; they have seen no bombs, no slaughter, no loss of homes and communities. They are comfortable, but they are not for the most part rich."

He scowled.

"If you emigrate to Canada expecting everything to

179

come to you easily, you will be a bad misfit. I say this because some of our people, not many, thank God, have gone with just that sort of idea and have been disappointed and disillusioned. It will take good hard work, faith, and the grace of God to make a start in any new land."

Maria watched the reaction of the other women, all of them deep in their own thoughts. Not one of them had anything less than profound respect for the office manager who, like themselves, had fled from country to country, and who had lost his own two sons in the war.

Herr Peters gave them one last searching look. "Just remember one thing, now and when you emigrate. Canada is not Heaven."

23

IT WAS ANOTHER delectable spring day. Twenty minutes before time for services to start Maria, Hansie, and Rosie, their heads bowed reverently, entered the building which the MCC had rented for church services, almost losing one another in the host of worshipers.

Starved for spiritual food and the warmth of Christian fellowship, the refugees filled the sanctuary far in advance of every service. They often started singing as much as half an hour before the meeting was scheduled to begin.

And this was no ordinary meeting, for it was a farewell service for the large group of men, women, and children who were finally to sail to far-off Paraguay on the *S.S. Charleton Monarch.*

Maria was glad that there were still a few seats to be had in the rear of the building. Although she was now steadily employed at potato peeling for the camp kitchen, she did not feel like standing. Rosie, crisp in the new dress assembled from the two old ones, snuggled close to Maria. Hansie, noticing that there were already women standing in the rear of the room, politely gave up his seat. Standing was no hardship for him.

"I'll meet you on the corner," he whispered huskily, and was gone before Maria had time to answer him.

It was then that the song leader, Herr Reimer, observing the rapidly filling hall, became restless to get the singing started. Standing behind the improvised pulpit he announced that the first song, while so many were still

181

coming in, would be *"Grosser Gott, wir loben Dich!"* Everyone leaned forward intently to catch the words as he read the first line, "Holy God, we praise Thy name; Lord of all, we bow before Thee." Then they sang the line after him. The lack of songbooks gave impetus to an old tradition of the Mennonites in the Ukraine to sing in this manner, the leader reading a line ahead of the singing.

Maria gazed around to see how many of the group sitting near her she could recognize as those who were to leave for Paraguay the following day. Some of her friends in the camp itself would be moving out tomorrow, and she had acquainted herself with a number of women who were living in the school building.

There was Frau Hamm in front of her. Maria felt sorry for her, partly crippled and with only one son left of her original family of three children. Frau Hamm had confided her troubles to Maria when they met in the park a few weeks before.

"My son is so skeptical," she had complained. "He was in a glum mood about the ship's having to be postponed, and I told him that prayer was all he could depend on. And then do you know what he said? 'Prayer hasn't helped me for a long time, Mother.' I tell you, that hurt me more than I can say." She had wiped her eyes. "If only he would find God and join the baptismal class before we leave!"

Beside Frau Hamm was a row of grandmothers whom Maria was certain she had seen at the temporary quarters. Imagine beginning a new life on another continent at the age of sixty, seventy, or more! And the MCC had made it clear that this life would not be easy, that there would be jungles to clear, Indians to befriend, houses to build, wells to dig, and gardens to plant.

Looking at Rosie by her side, Maria wondered if she and her children would pass the stiff physical examinations for entrance to Canada. After a number of interviews with the MCC, she had come to the conclusion that the letter from Tante Erika was the leading of God. Thus, they planned to go ahead with the processing for Canada. At the same time they hoped that should Hans later come to Gronau, he, too, could emigrate, since he had never been in the *S.S.*, but only in the regular German *Wehrmacht*. But if the door to Canada should close for them, what then? Could they, with the help of the rest of the colony, endure the hardships of frontier Paraguay? Maria would never take a step like that until she was sure that Hans was not somewhere in Germany.

A thrill crept up her spine as Maria thought of the three couples who would be united in Paraguay with the arrival of the *Charleton Monarch* and the trip inland to that little country. In all these cases one member had gone to Paraguay in 1947 on the ship *Volendam*, believing his or her partner to be dead. Now, through the efforts of the MCC, their spouses had been found and were coming to join them. It was not hard for Maria to imagine the dramatic reunion.

"Dear brothers and sisters in the Lord."

Maria's ponderings came to a hasty close, for the camp minister had ascended the platform with two of the MCC workers and was beginning the service.

"Dear brothers and sisters in the Lord," he began slowly, "we have come together to praise God and bid farewell to a large group among us, whom we have learned to love and for whom our prayers rise to our heavenly Father as they journey forth into the unknown future."

The aged minister adjusted his glasses and held his Bible up in a better position.

"But they do not go alone. Nor do any of us go alone, whether God takes us to Canada, or to the U.S.A., or to Paraguay, or should He will it that we remain in this land. For we have a Shepherd of our souls, a loving Father, a Guide and Comfort, a God in whom we can trust."

Brother Thiessen endeavored to hold his Bible a little more firmly, so that the audience would not notice his quivering hand. Then, through his tears, he read slowly and distinctly, in the beautiful Luther translation, the Twenty-third Psalm.

"Let us pray," he said simply, when he had finished the reading and glanced down at the tear-moistened eyes of the audience.

A heavy silence, save for a few audible sobs, filled the room as the faithful old minister prayed, his voice droning out words of intense gratitude for God's guiding providence in the past, for their safety at the moment, and for the hope which they had for the future, both temporally and eternally. Then he prayed for every individual who would leave their midst for the last lap of their long journey from the east to the sinking sun of the west, and for each family which would begin a new home in that faraway country. It was a long prayer, but no sound, not even the whimpering of a child, broke the awesome silence.

When Maria lifted her eyes after Brother Thiessen's

prayer, she saw that Frau Hamm and many other women were still praying. The members of the young people's choir had stood up from their places in the west corner of the building. She saw Elfrieda on the front row, her eyes fixed on the young man who stood before the group with arms upraised for the down beat of the first selection. And she saw Franz, too, on the back row, his dark eyes looking blacker because his face was so pale.

"When at last I am Home, when at last I am Home,
  Every storm will be over, when at last I am Home,"
the group sang softly, and as they hummed, the young director's clear tenor voice soloed the chorus. Always the choir was singing songs about Home, Maria thought. And they sang them with a wistful interpretation that only homeless refugees could put into the music.

Even the children were deeply touched. A little nine-year-old, who with her mother had been brought to camp to be emigrated with the group, tried to give a lovely poem that her mother had written for the occasion. But she only managed to get through the first two verses. The words, which described the heartaches of the trek and the loss of the child's father, were not difficult to memorize, but almost impossible for the child to recite.

As the program proceeded throughout the afternoon, MCC workers addressed the spellbound audience, repeating the experiences of groups whom they had transported earlier on the good ships *Volendam* and *General Stuart Heintzelmann*. They described the pioneer existence of the settlers and the need for faith in God and brotherly cooperation to make the new colonies successful. This land, the government of which had given permission to the MCC to bring in Mennonites, offered a safe haven to the long-persecuted refugees. It offered a hospitality which overcrowded Germany could not extend. Accommodations and transportation were primitive, but every man could at last, figuratively speaking, dwell under his own vine and fig tree. Mennonites, known the world over for their centuries of experiences in agriculture, had been promised freedom of conscience, even nonbearing of arms, if they would settle and tame the Chaco wilderness. But, as the MCC workers stressed, everything depended upon a sharing of burdens, brotherly love, and an unconquerable faith in God.

When the final prayer had been offered for the safekeeping of the departing wayfarers, Maria and Rosie were joined on the corner by a thoughtful Hansie. They decided to take the long way back to the *Klubhaus,* the path that led through the beautiful city park.

As they walked in silence, each absorbed in his own thoughts, Hansie suddenly blurted out, "Say, Mom, do we *have* to go to Canada?"

"Why, Son, we may not even be able to go, but don't you want to if we can?" she asked, surprised.

"Oh, I don't know. We've been studying about South America, and especially Paraguay, since so many were getting ready to go down there."

"Yes, Teacher said that she thinks we refugee children understand geography better than any other children our age, because we've been so many places and have so many connections," Rosie added proudly.

Maria smiled.

"But, Hansie, why do you want to go to Paraguay?"

"I don't know. I can't exactly say the reason in so many words."

He stuck his hand in his pocket and took on the casual mannerism he had picked up from Franz.

"It's just that I guess it takes a man to brave the wilderness down there. That's what Franz told me the other day. You know, Indians to befriend, and stumps to dig out, and wild animals to kill, and all sorts of adventure. I know I'd like it."

They had crossed the bridge spanning the river and were following the path through the small zoological section of the park. Stopping to admire the peacocks, Rosie asked, "Are there peacocks in Paraguay?"

"No—don't you remember, Rosie? Peacocks are from India. But there are lots of other birds and animals in Paraguay. I wish I could earn enough to buy a gun to take along, if we go."

Maria chuckled. She was afraid she did not share the boy's ambition to brave the wilderness of the Chaco. Not without Hans, at least. But she liked the evidences of manhood that she saw in her son since he began associating with Franz. She laughed privately at the way he walked like Franz, at the many times he quoted his older cousin, at the way he tried to control his changing voice.

"And you know, Mother," Rosie said, enjoying the opportunity to show off her own knowledge of a distant land, "they don't eat potatoes down there; they don't even grow them. They raise a plant called 'mandota' or something like that."

"Not 'mandota,' 'mandioca,' " Hansie corrected. "You get things so mixed—"

Abruptly Hans stopped, his hands propped on his hips.

'I'll say he's a woman hater; I'll say he's a woman hater!" he exclaimed in a shocked, disgusted tone. "Just look at them!"

But Franz and Elfrieda, hand in hand, never saw their audience; they seemed already to have been transplanted into another world.

24

THE DAY WAS A SAD ONE for Maria. When she arrived at Gronau and had been put to bed to rest for those first long months, Katharina had been in the bed next to her. Katharina, too, was discouragingly ill. She, too, was a refugee mother who had endured hardships and who had faint hopes of emigrating to Canada. But now Katharina was dead. She would not emigrate to a new home in America, for she had made the journey to her long Home.

Death, that old, familiar monster, had claimed another of Maria's friends. She had loved Katharina. They had talked together of many things; they had shared confidences. Today, however, Katharina's three little children, the oldest one only nine, sat silent and uncomprehending in the front row of the chapel.

The little edifice where they held the funeral services for Katharina sat sedately back from the road, semihidden by bushy trees, its tiny wooden framework symbolically constructed to point heavenward. From its outer walls, warmly clothed in lustrous ivy, to its rough but graceful interior, the chapel seemed to speak in soft, comforting words. Painted in gold letters in front of the room was the scriptural promise, "God is our refuge and strength, a very present help in trouble."

Softly Maria walked to the front of the chapel to look once more at the form of her friend. The unfinished casket, the scarcity of flowers, and the black crepe paper

189

dress, trimmed with a white collar, gave evidence that the homeless woman had died in poverty. But Maria, remembering Katharina's unselfish spirit, knew that her friend had been rich toward God.

Again the young people's choir sang songs of Home, as they had done a few days previous at the farewell service for the *Charleton Monarch*. But this time it was different; the words took on new meaning. Could it be, Maria wondered, that refugees spent too much time dreaming over their past and future homes on earth, to the point where they forgot about their eternal Home? Home, after all, is not merely structural, she thought; it is wherever your loved ones are. The tears came as she remembered that most of her dear ones were in Heaven—her mother, her father, her brother and sisters perhaps, and then Lenie. Hans? No—she felt sure that he was alive. But where?

Katharina's death seemed indeed untimely; had not a great tragedy come to her, she would have been caring for her children for many years to come. But, as Maria remembered her, Katharina had been an old woman. Lying in the camp hospital, she had described the tragic day on the trek when she had so nearly frozen to death. Since that time she had been but a shadow of her real self, the person she so much longed to be.

Maria had dreaded this service, for funerals were hard for the refugee, bringing back into sharp focus scenes that time had blurred, opening wounds once more that time had seemingly healed. But after the minister had read the jubilant words of hope in the resurrection from I Corinthians 15, Maria felt comforted. She had almost forgotten that "death is swallowed up in victory."

Forming a long procession behind the horse-drawn hearse, they walked the quarter mile of gravel road to the cemetery, passing the large Lutheran church. As was customary, the church bells began ringing as soon as the funeral procession was within a hundred feet of the church. The graveside services were not long, and Maria began to look for a companion for the walk homeward.

She had noticed the woman in the chapel and had wondered why she was alone. Seeing that the friends she had come with were no longer there and that this stoop-shouldered stranger was only a few yards ahead, Maria hurried to catch up.

"May I walk with you, seeing you are alone?" she asked, smiling through the tears that were still in her eyes.

The woman glanced up at her, surprised.

"Oh, I guess, if you want to."

"Why, of course I do." She had emphasized the "want" in such an odd way that Maria had the feeling she should reassure her.

"I know that I have seen you several times, but I can't think who you are. What is your name?"

"Taisa Braun. I don't get out very much. My son Anton usually goes for our food. My husband works in the factory. I have been assigned some sewing that I ordinarily do in my room. That's why you don't see me so often, I guess."

"How old is your little boy? I have a son, too."

"He's fourteen, but he's only in the fifth grade. Had to stop school too often, couldn't keep up."

"I know how that is." Maria smiled at the woman

again, noticing that she spoke a very broken German and seemed miserably uncomfortable and self-conscious. But Frau Braun did not return the smile. Instead she continued almost as though she were talking to herself.

"He hates being in the same class with children so much younger than he is. He's little for his age, but it still makes him angry. The teacher doesn't like him, either."

It was then that it dawned on Maria who Frau Braun was. Only this morning, when the conversation around the potato kettle had deteriorated to gossip, the Brauns had been up for discussion. He was a Mennonite, but had married a non-Mennonite Russian woman. The woman, they said, was shiftless and unfriendly. Maria had been ashamed of the unkind things that had been said about her.

"Fräulein Bartel seems like such a nice teacher. Perhaps if you got better acquainted with her—"

Frau Braun shrugged her shoulders. They had come to the *Klubhaus* and she turned to go to her room by way of the veranda.

"I don't get acquainted very easily. You are all Mennonites. You have your own dialect; I cannot understand nor speak it. You have your own customs. I do not understand them. So I am not one of you."

And without another word, she was gone.

Looking after her helplessly, thinking what she should have said, Maria did not notice her son until he tapped her on her elbow.

"Mom! Don't you know who that is? My goodness, Mother, why are you talking to her?"

"Why, that was Frau Braun. What in the world do you mean?"

She gazed down into his stubborn eyes and saw that she was in for an argument. And surely the street corner was no place to stage a verbal battle if there had to be one. She led the way to their room.

"She's Anton Braun's mother. She's a Russian, too. And Anton is the worst fellow in the class. He doesn't cooperate; he teases the girls; he—"

Maria had had enough. She could do little about discrimination against this poor woman, but she was not going to have such unkindness in her own family.

"Now listen, Son. There is nothing wrong with Frau Braun that a little kindness won't help. She needs a friend and someday I am going to go over and make a call. And what is more, you ought to be nice to Anton."

Rosie had entered, had listened curiously, and could no longer be quiet.

"I'll tell you why Hansie doesn't like Anton. I'll tell you. The teacher put him next to Irmgart and—"

Hansie lunged forward, grabbing one of Rosie's braids in his fist, but she continued.

"Irmgart and Anton talk in class and today he walked her home."

She darted out the blanket entrance, Hansie close behind her. "That's why he doesn't like him. That's the whole, terrible truth."

25

"Now, ROSIE, start all over again. You were downtown and you thought you saw whom?"

Maria knelt beside the humped-up form, stroking the fuzzy braids, trying gently to unearth the face that was buried in the dark blanket.

"Whom did you see, ROSIE?"

"Him. Papa!"

"Rosie! Where? Where did you see him?"

"I didn't."

"But you just said you did."

"I—I thought I saw him. He looked just like Papa from the back. I got so excited I chased him for a whole block."

She stopped to heave a deep sigh.

"Oh, I'm so-o-o em—embarrassed! I ran up to him and called him. But it wasn't Papa at all. He turned around and looked at me as though I were crazy."

"And then what did you do?"

"I just started to cry. I couldn't help it. I've never been so disappointed. He just stood watching me while I ran crying down the street. It was awful."

Maria put her arms around Rosie and searched for words to comfort her. How many times she herself had stared at faces on the street, ever on the lookout for Hans. Surely no one knew better than she what it was like to think you saw him until the second look revealed a total stranger. But she knew she would continue searching faces as long as it took to find him, just as Herr and Frau Peters never ceased looking for their two sons, and just as many others in camp kept watching and hoping.

They sat talking together until Rosie, unburdened, began to comb her hair for supper, looking in the little piece of mirror she had found one day on her way to school.

"Say, Mom!" There was a bulge in the blanket entrance and Hansie stuck his face through the opening.

"Mamma, Franz wants me to go for a walk with him. He wants to show me a chimney sweep who is cleaning a chimney near the park."

He turned and motioned to the older boy to come in. Franz sat down on the proffered chair, crossed his legs, and gazed admiringly at his "little sister," as he liked to call Rosie. Seeing her swollen eyes, he looked at Maria.

"Rosie has had a disappointment this afternoon," Maria explained, as though he had asked the question audibly. "She thought she saw her papa."

She hesitated, then added, "There have been many times that I have had the same experience. But there is still hope. Sometime when we think we see him, it might really be him."

"Hansie, let's take Rosie along to the park," Franz said, rising to go.

"Aw, Franz." It was Hansie's turn to be disappointed. "Do we have to? It's bad enough that you're always with Frieda; I never get to see you much any more. Now that we can go, you want to take a girl along."

"But you walk Irmgart home from school. You don't mind girls that much," Rosie piped up.

"That's right. And you don't want to be selfish with

Franz, Hansie. Other people like to be with him, too," Maria laughed.

"And you can't blame him for wanting to be with Elfrieda." Rosie's voice floated out loud and clear.

"Sh-h-h, Rosie." Maria was afraid that half a dozen pairs of ears were catching Rosie's remark.

"Did I hear my name?"

There was a merry laugh, and Elfrieda appeared through the door. Then there was an awkward moment; she hadn't known that Franz was there.

But the moment was short. Suddenly Maria and Elfrieda were alone, Frieda still blushing a pretty pink.

"You two are together a lot, Frieda," Maria said when the three were gone. "Hansie is just a little jealous of you lately. I think he was under the impression that he owned Franz until the day we saw you two strolling home from the farewell service."

"I'm sorry, Maria. But the way Franz talks, he still sees pretty much of his 'brother.' "

"It's all right. I wasn't really serious. We all feel pretty proud of the match, because you both are so much a part of us."

Elfrieda flushed again, and love made her beautiful. "That's nice of you, Maria."

Then she sobered, as she stretched out on Rosie's cot.

"It's kind of you, but sometimes I wish I had never seen Franz."

Maria had picked up one of Rosie's stockings to darn. Now she dropped it in her lap, watching Elfrieda, waiting for her to go on.

The girl closed her eyes and rubbed her forehead as though she were plagued with a bad headache.

196

"It was all so perfect, so very perfect until this happened. Herta and I and Abram and Mother and little Sarah, all reunited miraculously. All of us going to Saskatchewan, Canada, together. Now—"

"You mean that if you should marry Franz, they would go to Saskatchewan and you would go to Ontario with Franz?"

"I didn't say I was going to marry Franz, Maria. He hasn't even asked me—yet. But since I work in the office, I found out today that Franz is not going to Ontario. Maria, Franz didn't pass the Canadian officials."

Her words were full of pity.

"I can't tell him. I don't want to be anywhere around when he finds out. Oh, Maria, I feel so sorry for him."

Maria was at a loss to know what to say.

"God is also in Paraguay, Frieda."

"Yes, but my mother and brother and sisters won't be."

"You've given yourself away, my dear. Your pity is not all directed toward Franz."

Elfrieda grinned through her tears.

"I'm so glad I have you to talk to, Maria," she said. "I haven't had the heart to tell this to the folks. And I'm so mixed up. I never knew that I would ever get in such a predicament."

Maria sat in silence, for she realized that Elfrieda wanted understanding from her more than counsel. She remembered how they had met in Poland, and how they had learned to know one another almost as well as if they had been sisters.

Time had dragged during those days at the Stony City camp, for there was nothing to do, living quarters were stuffy and crowded, and there was continual fear of the constantly advancing **Communist** army. One day they had been sitting together in a corner of the large, ugly room, and Elfrieda had told them all about her past.

Born in a beautiful little village in the Ukraine, Elfrieda's early childhood had been happy and normal. She could remember going barefoot with her mother to a large, attractive Mennonite church. She remembered celebrating Christmas and exchanging gifts.

But the year 1930 marked the beginning of a bad time for her, as it did for all of them. Churches were closed, preachers were *verschleppt* to Siberia, land was confiscated, property turned over to the *Kollectiv*, and friends and relatives sent north to work.

Elfrieda's grandparents on her mother's side were sent away, but those on her father's side stayed with them, living on the scanty rations of the family because there were no old people's pensions any more. Since Elfrieda's parents, like all other adults, were required to work long hours in the *Kollectiv*, the old people cared for the children. An aged saint, Elfrieda's grandfather refused to give up his faith. Until the day he died he secretly read Scripture and taught the children to sing and pray.

They kept hoping that it wouldn't happen to them. So many other fathers had been dragged from their weeping families. But it did. On March 21, 1938, at 2:00 A.M. an auto drove up to the house and a man knocked, not on the door, but on the window.

"Get ready—you have to go fast," the heartless voice called, and crying did no good. Mother packed a quick lunch and Papa whispered in her ear, "Pray for me; perhaps the dear Saviour will return me to you."

Then he went away in the wagon, never to be seen or

heard from again. Everyone wept in his bed; gloom hung heavy over them all. Mother leaned hard on the Lord, knelt with Grandmother, and prayed long into the morning. A baby was coming, a frail little thing that managed to live in spite of it all.

The years following were difficult. Mother continued to work hard. Elfrieda wanted to go to high school but couldn't.

It was in 1941 that the German-Russian war broke out and all men between sixteen and sixty-four were evacuated, walking under police guards. On October 2, in one hour, all German-speaking women and children, between seven and eight thousand, were loaded with their luggage and taken to the railway station. Watched by the Communists, they sang Christian songs to keep up their spirits. Four fearful days and nights they lay in the station, the Germans coming closer. Light flashed into the station from the nearby fields. When the Communists, on the fifth day, were pushed back, the women and children were permitted to return to their homes.

Elfrieda, during this time, had not been at the terminal with the others. She had been forced to dig trenches in another part of the country. When she finally returned to her home and saw that her people were still there, a wonderful reunion followed.

"We no longer need to pray for Elfrieda. Now we need fear only for Papa," they had said.

With the Germans occupying their territory, a new life began. But the good period was short-lived. On September 11, 1943, Elfrieda, along with thousands of other German-speaking people, fled in the wake of the German Army westward. Thus began the long, wearisome trek, the miles of aching travel, frosted feet, and fatal illnesses. Making the last lap of the journey by train, the family finally arrived in a refugee camp on the Polish border, where they were quartered for the winter.

Again by train, Elfrieda and her family were next sent to Stony City, where, despite the difference in their ages, Maria and Elfrieda became close friends. Maria stayed there until the Communists again closed in, but Elfrieda and her mother had gone on by that time and had settled themselves farther west, hoping that this move would be their last. Her mother and aunt working on a farm, the little child in school, her sister away at agricultural school, and her brother stationed a number of miles away on a farm, Elfrieda determined once more to go to school. Thus she enrolled in a secretarial course. One last happy Christmas the family spent together, but on January 10, 1945, they separated once more.

And then it happened again. The Communists were coming; there was nothing to do but flee. Hoping to return to study again, Elfrieda packed her goods and her food on a wagon and fled with the other students ahead of the advancing army. They had no overshoes, and their feet became blistered, but the cannons roared behind them and they trudged wearily onward. With her mother only ten kilometers away, Elfrieda felt that she must go to her, but there was no time. Taking a train to Berlin, the entire school determined to stay together and went on to the South German Alps, where they were finally sent out to work for farmers.

It was no wonder, Maria thought, that Elfrieda could scarcely bear thinking of another separation from her family. For locating them had been long and trying.

Most people were not so fortunate as she. Finding her sister Herta in the American Zone, Elfrieda had accompanied her to the British Zone, where they had a frightening encounter with Communist officials who urged them to return to their homeland. Secretly hoping to get across the Dutch border, they immediately left for Gronau, where they found crossing the border impossible.

That is where the MCC had come in. For many other Mennonites, like Elfrieda, knowing that their forefathers who settled the Ukraine were originally from Holland, had tried unsuccessfully to cross into the Netherlands. So many had come to Gronau with this hope, in fact, that when their American brethren discovered them, they set up a camp for those who had congregated there. From this camp they worked out into the western zones.

Herta and Elfrieda had managed to keep in contact with their mother and baby sister, who were still having a trying time in Poland. Abram, who had slipped across the border into the British Zone, was also corresponding with their mother. When he found out his sisters were in Gronau, he joined them. Anxious about their mother, the three discussed their problem with the MCC. The MCC representative in Poland was contacted and through his help Elfrieda's mother finally arrived in Germany. Elfrieda was thrilled whenever she thought of how her family, with the exception of her father, was together once more.

Remembering Elfrieda's past, Maria looked at the young woman on the cot and felt desperately sorry for her. Happiness seemed for her like a bright-colored toy held in front of a baby and snatched away just as the child would almost have it in his grasp.

"Don't you see, Maria, what this means?" Elfrieda asked at length, her face stormy with the struggle that raged within her.

"The trouble is that we love each other. I love Franz, and I don't mind admitting it—to you. Franz will quickly adjust to making a home in Paraguay. He is strong and sure of himself and courageous. But after all these troublesome years of trying to keep our family together an ocean and a continent will still lie between us."

Elfrieda sat up, poised on the edge of the cot, and Maria put her arm around her.

"I know why he hasn't proposed to me, Maria. It is because he was uncertain about his future and he knew what he would be asking of me. But it will come, and soon."

26

THE DAY HUNG LOW and gloomy over the drab army barracks that Hans called home. Discouraged and downcast, he lay on the bunk and nursed his backache. He suspected that were he able to find a job, that backache would disappear in a moment, for the uncertainty of things since he had come to the government camp in Kassel was far more difficult than a heavy day's work.

Two months had passed since Hans had successfully crossed the border "black," but still he had no job. The refugee, unneeded and unwanted in a crowded society, was the last to be hired and the first to be fired. His companions in misery, bored and aimless, stood around in the halls, shuffled in and out of the rooms, and grumbled to themselves and one another.

Yesterday it had been worse. Several rooms up the hall there had been a knife fight between two men who had a little too much to drink. And those men had been fathers, with their helpless wives and children looking on. What right had they to have their children with them, so undeserving they were of their good luck? How unjust God was, if there was a God, to snatch a fine woman like Maria away to an earthly Hell, and at the same time let other families hang together, though they bickered among themselves and though the men beat their wives and neglected their children.

Of course, they weren't all that way. Hans had to admit that there were numerous families who tried desperately to maintain their sanity and integrity, in spite of the living conditions in which they were forced to exist.

There was Frau Burkert across the aisle from him, a young widow with two little children. It was difficult to retain one's self-respect when one had to live in an uncurtained room with twenty other miscellaneously assorted people of both sexes and all ages. Yet she attempted to care for her children and disregard curious stares of men like August, who lived in the bunk above Hans. Hans wished August would let her alone.

Across from Hans' bunk and several feet from Frau Burkert lived an aged couple; Hans didn't know their names. But through the endless days and nights they entertained one another, taking long, slow walks up and down the halls. Hans had long ago concluded that the old man was feeble-minded, for some of the less thoughtful inmates enjoyed repeating his ofttimes nonsensical remarks.

On the other side of the old couple sat a family in no little distress. Herr Reutzel, had he lived in normal times, had not his home been destroyed by bombers while he fought on the battlefields of Russia, would have been a respectable man. But moral and Christian principles, taken for granted in good times, were sometimes disregarded entirely in wartime. Herr Reutzel, like so many others, felt that right and wrong must give way to expediency when one's family was hungry. Thus, he had only recently been released from prison, where he had spent a year for stealing a typewriter and selling it on the black market to buy food for his wife and children. He was determined now to "go straight" again, but he was finding it increasingly difficult to get a job.

His wife sat across from him, diapering their baby with a ragged bit of curtain material. The child had been born just before he went to prison.

Hans felt sorry for the children in camp. Games and toys were scarce and the yard was bleak and barren, a mud hole in wet weather. Books were indeed rare, good ones almost unobtainable.

Many of the children arrived in camp with lice and bedbugs; scabies, impetigo, and other skin diseases; and with teeth decayed to rotten stumps. They had been pushed around all their lives, and scores of them had lost one or both of their parents. As a result they were pouty and disagreeable, jealous and unsociable. There were many fits of coughing and much crying.

Feeling his cot vibrate, Hans dodged two heavy feet which suddenly descended from the bunk above him. Then he lay back on the cot, pretending to be asleep.

Glad as he was to escape from the Eastern Zone into American-occupied territory, Hans hadn't quite bargained for this. For from the first day he set foot in the city of Kassel, 85 per cent destroyed, a city of ruins, he had been increasingly aware that he was still an unwanted refugee, a wanderer without family ties, friends, employment, or security of any kind. Making his way through the acres and acres of twisted steel and pulverized brick, he had reported to a refugee center and had been assigned a bunk in a camp on the outskirts of town. There he awaited an assignment, perhaps clearing away rubble or cleaning bricks, which never came.

The owner of the feet from the bunk above shook himself and charged a knowing look at Hans.

"Say, you look like you just buried your grandmother," he observed. "What you need, fellow, is a woman."

He shot an insinuating glance toward Frau Burkert, who was busy spooning a last gulp of soup into her youngest. The woman, carefully avoiding any change of facial expression, got up and hurried from the room, carrying one child and dragging the other.

"I'm married," Hans answered curtly. "I've told you that before."

"So what! Are you going to live in a dream castle all the rest of your life with a woman who is most likely dead? And what if she isn't? You've got a right to get something out of life. God knows it's dull enough around here."

It was no use. Hans decided to escape the same way Frau Burkert had, by way of the open door into the dusty hall. Today a load of foul-smelling fish had come in, but what would ordinarily have been obnoxious was most welcome to the never-satisfied appetites of the camp inmates.

What kept him from doing like the rest? Hans wondered to himself as he strode down the hall, trying to escape from his own thoughts as well as the man, August. There were times when he almost felt like making up to that poor widow across the aisle, both to save her from August and to ease his own loneliness. She wasn't bad-looking and Hans honestly liked her. But in his heart he knew the answer. It was Maria. Her memory kept him not only from committing physical suicide, but moral suicide as well. On one hand, it was because of her and the children, the impossibility of coming to their rescue, the torture of his loneliness, that he often felt like ending it all. But paradoxically it was because of Maria that he could not do it.

Hans passed a group of children in the hall. They were young delinquents who spent the endless time at their disposal in the only ways they knew how, by devising their own entertainment, dealing in the black market, picking up cigarette stubs from the streets, getting into trouble. His heart ached for them, for in them he saw Hansies and Rosies. Were his own children in even worse circumstances?

Surely there would be a job for him tomorrow! Maybe they had overlooked his application. In his restlessness Hans decided to walk through some of the other barracks. Anything for a change!

They were all very much the same, though, those barracks. Long colorless halls, with faces peering from the adjoining dormitory rooms—young faces, old faces, tired faces, a few hopeful ones.

Suddenly Hans stopped with a jolt. Could he believe what he heard? Almost he would have thought it was Rosie, that thin, flutelike voice, speaking in his native *Platt.* His heart racing, Hans peered through the door of a dormitory room, empty except for one family already eating their supper in a far corner. A middle-aged couple and a boy in his teens stood and sat around the table, intent on what the child was saying.

There was no doubt about it. They were Mennonites, Mennonites, Mennonites! Friends! No one he had ever met, to be sure, but simple, honest, lovable people like his Maria, Hans, and Rosie.

"May I interrupt?" he asked in *Platt,* clearing his throat to announce his presence. "I am so delighted to find some other Mennonites here. I was desperately, miserably lonesome."

The older man jumped to his feet, clasped Hans' hand in his equally firm one, and ushered him to their only remaining chair.

"Wonderful, wonderful, wonderful!" he exclaimed, striking his hands together with fervor.

Hans introduced himself briefly, while the father stroked his mustache, the mother stacked the dishes and began unraveling the string from an old sack, and the children looked on in silent interest.

"We are the David Martens family from Marienthal, and this is my wife Eva, our son David, and our daughter Eunice," the father continued, as spokesman for the shier members of his family.

He grew sober for a long moment, and his wife's eyes filled with tears.

"We had two other daughters older than David, but they are lost."

There was another drawn-out silence, and when Hans looked up all eyes were focused on his face.

"Do you have a family?" Martens asked simply, and his voice wavered with apprehension as though he already sensed from his manner what Hans' answer would be.

Hans looked squarely at the older Martens, and his mouth twitched.

"I had a wife and three children only a year and a half ago. We were very happy. Then while I took our youngest to the hospital the Russians kidnapped Maria, ten-year-old Hans, and eight-year-old Rosie. Meanwhile Lenie died. So I am alone."

Hans was sorry he had unbared his own grief when he

looked at Martens' wife. He needed sympathy, Hans thought, but not at the expense of another whose sorrow was just as great.

"I'm sorry," he apologized clumsily, "you have enough troubles of your own."

"Don't be sorry," Eva assured him quickly, and he noticed that she had the kind of pluck that Maria always had. "We understand. It helps us all to share our burdens."

"You would have been very much interested in our guests last week, speaking of sharing burdens," Martens said, his face lighting up with pleasure. Placing his hand on Hans' knee, Martens asked, "Did you know that we have brethren in the United States and Canada, folks who have heard of our distress and are trying to help us?"

"No!" Hans was almost too amazed to answer.

"Yes! Several of their representatives were here last week. Their name was Warkentin and they spoke our native *Platt,* although with a strange accent, of course."

"Quite a different accent, but easy to understand," young David added, leaning forward in his enthusiasm.

"But—but how did they know you were here?"

"We had some correspondence with relatives in the British Zone. They had come into contact with some of this American relief committee's workers. The Mennonite Central Committee—that's what our brethren from America call themselves—were distributing food and clothing to the German populace when they ran across the Mennonite refugees. They asked if our cousins knew of any other Mennonites anywhere and they gave them our names. Then when the Warkentins came down our way, they looked us up."

"What were these Warkentins like? What do they propose to do for us?" Hans' heart raced with the thought of any kind of help—help to get a job, help to get out of this wretched camp, a little extra food.

"They were an elderly couple who were sent here to minister to the refugees spiritually," the older Martens replied thoughtfully.

"And that they did," Eva added quietly, taking a new black Bible from a box under the table.

"You mean that they came all the way across the ocean just to hand out Bibles?" Hans could not hide his disappointment. Why, he already owned a Bible, and little good it did him, though he had carried it with his belongings ever since he left Frau Schmidt back in Krauter. He had only read it once, and seeing that it was of little help, he had never bothered with it again.

Eva looked at Hans significantly.

"Oh, no, that's not all, though that would have been enough if they had come just for that," she replied.

"They explained it all to us," young David continued earnestly. "First they came over to Europe 'in the name of Christ' to distribute food and clothing to war victims and to help in any other way they could. It wasn't long until they discovered a number of our brethren in northern Germany trying to get across the border into Holland. When they found out how many of us there are, thousands of us, they set up a camp at Gronau in the British Zone."

"And now they have another camp at Backnang in the American Zone," old David interrupted.

"Yes, and from these camps they try to help the scattered refugees in any way they can. They can only take

210

so many into camp and they said they would keep us in mind and try either to take us in sometime or place us on a farm close to Gronau."

"But you are forgetting the most important part, Son," the father interrupted again. "Although what they can do for us materially is limited, they are attempting to help us emigrate to new homes in Canada if possible, some to the U.S.A., and the rest to Paraguay. It is unbelievable."

And unbelievable it seemed to Hans, as he listened while the Martens tried to remember every word of the conversation. They described to him how the MCC was trying to find American and Canadian sponsors for some of the Mennonites, sending others, such as lumbermen, farm workers, or industrial workers, to Canada under Workers' Schemes.

"Has not the Lord been very good to us, Brother?" Martens asked, as he sat fondling the new Bible the Warkentins had given them. "And we are so unworthy of His great and marvelous benefits."

Bitterness, so long rooted in Hans' heart, sprang forth in his words before he could check them.

"What benefits? I guess we should thank the Lord for robbing us of our homes, our wives, our children, our sanity! I guess we should praise Him for allowing our cities to be burned, our land to be drenched with blood, our women to be ravished, our children to be turned into hateful little thieves. I guess—"

Martens leaned forward, looking squarely at Hans.

"And why, may I ask, do you blame God for the mess that this world is in?"

Hans lifted his face and met the challenge.

"Because if I believe in a God, it must be a God of love. He would not allow the injustices I have seen in my lifetime. He simply would not allow them. Maria believed in Him, and what good did it do her? I do not believe there is a God."

"But you have forgotten one thing, Hans," Martens replied calmly, calling him by his Christian name for the first time. "You have forgotten that there is another force beside God in our universe, a diabolical force. You dare not hold God responsible for Satan's work."

He opened the Book that lay in his lap.

"I want you to listen to several passages which have helped us struggle through the kind of doubts that have overtaken you."

He began to read:

"Why do the heathen rage, and the people imagine a vain thing?
The kings of the earth set themselves, and the rulers take counsel together, against the Lord, and against his anointed, saying,
Let us break their bands asunder, and cast away their cords from us.
He that sitteth in the heavens shall laugh:
    the Lord shall have them in derision.
Then shall he speak unto them in his wrath,
    and vex them in his sore displeasure."

He paused in his reading and looked again at Hans.

"God is not finished with the world yet, Hans. He is just biding His time. Another place it says, 'Vengeance is mine; I will repay, saith the Lord.'

"And now, I want you to hear another passage, which

is our hope. Brother and Sister Warkentin read it to us when they were here, and we have reread it many times since:

> 'And ye shall hear of wars and rumours of wars:
>   see that ye be not troubled:
> For all these things must come to pass,
>   but the end is not yet.
> For nation shall rise against nation,
>   and kingdom against kingdom:
> And there shall be famines, and pestilences, and earth-
>   quakes, in divers places.
> All these are the beginning of sorrows. . . .
> But he that shall endure unto the end, the same shall
>   be saved.'

"These are the words of our Lord."

Hans looked around at the family group and he knew that they, too, had known sorrow, that they had experienced the same grievous things that he had had to endure. Yet within them was no thought of defeat. They were like that verse Maria had said that night, something about being persecuted but not forsaken. That was all he could recall. In his misery he had several times wished he could remember more of it, but he did not know how to look up the verse.

He wished he had what the Martens had. But it could never be. All of a sudden the atmosphere seemed close, stuffy, and for some reason he wanted to run, to get away from these well-meaning people and their faith. Inexplicably, he felt cornered.

"I really ought to go," he said haltingly, pretending to rise, but remaining half-seated. "But first, I'd like to ask you, do you think this Mennonite Central Committee would help me to emigrate? I'm not a very good Mennonite, when it comes to faith, but I'm not too bad otherwise."

"We'll give the address to you," old Martens replied kindly.

Hans continued thinking aloud. "If I could get a job, perhaps in a few months I could pay my train fare to Gronau after I have bought a pair of shoes."

This time he really rose to go.

"It's been wonderful meeting you. I may come back."

Old Martens took his hand. "By all means, do, friend. And—and if you'd like to borrow our Bible to read, you are welcome to do so."

What was there about this family that made him feel so wretched? Hans fingered his collar nervously. "I have one of my own, but I've seldom bothered to read it."

"You have a Bible and you're not reading it? Please," Martens clutched Hans' arm firmly, "please promise us you'll begin, if only a little at a time. You cannot afford to live without it."

Why did he promise? Hans wondered on his way back to his barracks. Was it the sincerity of the Martenses or his own inner misery that cried for relief? He could not say. But he did know that tonight he would unpack his Testament and begin reading, though it was hard to see how it would ever help in his wretched loneliness.

27

IF ELFRIEDA'S EVERYDAY FACE usually glowed, her wedding day countenance was resplendent with happiness. Yet, beneath the serenity and graciousness of her bearing, Maria knew that there lingered a hidden sorrow, a pity for the middle-aged woman in the audience who was her mother.

Elfrieda had battled for days with a gnawing desire to stay with her family. She had seemed faraway and remote when Maria talked with her. But one day the two of them, Elfrieda and Franz, had come hand in hand to announce their new relationship. And Maria noticed that peace rested on the face of her friend. The girl Elfrieda had overnight become a woman.

"Did I say my part all right?" Rosie queried, when Maria and the children returned to their room to take off their good clothes.

"I told you, Rosie," Maria replied warmly, "that you did very well. Perhaps you did say your poem a little too fast, but that's the way we all do when we get excited. Really, Rosie, I was happy!"

"Didn't she look beautiful?" Rosie had mentioned Elfrieda's dress half a dozen times on the way back to the *Lager* from the hall where the ceremony had been performed. And it was true that the rented white gown which Frieda wore could not have fitted her better had it been her own. Maria had helped her alter the gown a little in the waist, but they had been careful not to dam-

215

age it in any way, since it had to be returned to the shop as soon as they were finished with it.

"Did you like Brother Thiessen's sermon, children?" Maria asked. They had discussed everything about the simple but impressive ceremony, from the songs the choir rendered, to the pine-decorated chairs in which the wedding couple sat during the service. But they had not discussed the earnest words which Brother Thiessen had spoken to the pair.

Rosie giggled. "Honestly, Mother, I didn't hear a thing Brother Thiessen said. I was just all the time saying my poem over and over in my head. I was too scared to think of anything else."

Maria smiled. One of the customs connected with a Mennonite wedding in Russia was that little girls or older friends would recite poetry of good wishes to the couple immediately following the ceremony. Rosie and Frieda's little sister, Sarah, had been given this honor, and both girls were thrilled. Maria had felt sorry for Sarah though, for, realizing the separation this marriage would mean for their family, she had been unable to finish her recitation.

All this time Hansie had been silent, too silent. Maria had noticed it all the way home and now that the boy sat dully uncommunicative in his corner, she felt she should probe through the thin shell of his reserve.

"Hansie, what's bothering you? You act as though you have been to a funeral instead of a wedding."

"Yes, what is the matter with you anyhow?" Rosie asked.

"Now, Rosie, you keep quiet. You always want to have your nose in everything."

216

"What is it, Hansie?"

The boy stared dismally at the row of cups and plates across the cubicle from where he sat.

"It's just that everything goes wrong at once. Franz goes and gets married and you have to go back to the hospital and—"

"I hope I won't have to be in the hospital long this time." Maria was determined not to cry, and the aggravating lump that wouldn't stay swallowed annoyed her.

"It's for our good in the long run, children. Herr Peters said that if I can just get built up, maybe I'll pass the physical the next time the Canadian officials come. We have a lot to be thankful for that you children are in such good shape."

"I know," Hansie replied, "but what are Rosie and I going to do while you're gone?"

"The *Hausvater* just told me today, children, that you will probably live with the Guenthers. They are an older couple without children. And, of course, Hansie, you will look after Rosie and be a real brother to her."

Maria grinned and gave his ear a playful pull. "You know, you quarrel with Rosie when we're alone, but just let anyone else say anything about your sister, and you are her best friend."

Yet, that night, when the lights were out and Maria lay awake on her cot, she did not feel so sure. What might happen to the children while she was hospitalized? That she had failed to pass the physical requirements for entrance to Canada, and that she had once more to be separated from her family, was hard for her to understand.

She did not need to worry about Rosie. Conscientious

and punctual, Rosie would roll out of bed on time, wash her face, braid her own hair, and keep her lessons up to date.

But it was different with Hansie. Good, nutritious food and the stability of the camp environment had helped to make him the husky, unpredictable boy that he was intended to be. Never were two days alike when one lived with him, for he was both curious and impulsive, and his inquisitive disposition sometimes led him to investigate matters which were most assuredly none of his business.

And to make matters more difficult, there was this foolish triangle. To Hansie's chagrin, Rosie kept Maria posted on which of the boys, Anton or Hansie, had walked Irmgart home from school. Then Hansie would say very uncomplimentary things about the little half-Russian chap. He still had not forgiven Maria for befriending Anton's ostracized mother.

It would be different were not Franz married. Even then Maria would have called Franz and Elfrieda in and asked them to keep an eye on the boy, but Elfrieda's family was to sail for Canada in only two weeks, probably never to see the young couple again. It would not be fair to take any of their precious time.

Maria's faith had come a long way since that terrible night in Kornrade when she had learned of Lenie's death; when she had battled it out on her knees, finally surrendering Lenie to God; when she, like Job, had accepted the higher wisdom of a loving heavenly Father. Never again had she jaywalked so far from the path of trustful dependence upon God as she did that night in Kornrade. Yet, there were times, like tonight, when she found it hard to lay her hand in God's, to turn over everything to Him and let Him overrule her desires according to His own good pleasure.

And then she knew where her trouble lay.

It was her own persistent will again.

She had not surrendered.

Her heart was set on Canada— the home they would make while waiting for Hans to come—the farmer Rosie would marry—the education Hansie would get—the new clothes they would all have. A real home, security, stability, rest.

She had never surrendered this hope to God.

Nor had she surrendered her present to His faithful hands. Fear, like the mercury in a thermometer, went up in camp whenever world conditions looked especially ominous. Maria had to admit that she had allowed herself to be influenced by the hysteria of some of her neighbors.

Would not the God who had watched over her until this day continue to care for her and her children? Again, she recalled Herr Peters' wise words, "Canada is not Heaven." You could not run off and escape from yourself in Canada, for you would have to take your own miserable, doubting self wherever you went. If she could not trust God in a refugee camp in postwar Germany, Maria knew that she would not be able to live by faith in a new world.

Perhaps her impatience in waiting for Hans was also part of her trouble. Not a day passed that she did not pray for his coming. The thought that he might have gone into Siberia to look for her was so dreadful that she had been afraid to face the possibility of it. It was time that she stopped closing her mind to this fear and faced it squarely. For they had been here almost a year, and the MCC had never been able to find a trace of her husband anywhere. His love for his family may have driven him to give his life in an attempt to save them.

Suddenly Maria sat up in her bed. Worry after all was a failure to face reality. Had God ever given her any experience without the grace to bear it? He had not, and He would not.

Closing her eyes, Maria lay back in the everlasting arms of her Father, a new peace settling over her being. She would live one day at a time, with God; she would stop dodging her fears and would face them.

Her sleep was sweet.

28

To the school children, who practiced their parts each day for the most wonderful season of the year, Christmas did seem a long time in coming. To many of them, it was their first *real* Christmas. For Mariechen, the little curlyhead now reciting her piece, her face a study in childish excitement, seven tragic Christmases had passed, each sadly lacking in peace and good will toward men. And for the tiny blond Dietrich, life seemed just to have begun. Mentally he went over the difficult part again, always mindful of the large audience who would hear his discourse on the shepherds. Little would one have guessed that only two months before Dietrich and his mother had shivered from cold and fright in a miserable hovel, where they had been shelved by a selfish farmer.

Children have good forgetters. A look into the schoolroom, where the refugee children were practicing for the great week, revealed the joy and expectancy that is found in the faces of children everywhere during the Christmas season.

Hansie bent over the part he was to play, reviewing precisely the great drama with which he would voice his,

"Go and search diligently for the young child; and when ye have found him—"

The part of a wicked man intrigued his soul, for, though he had every intention of being good like his mother, this role gave vent to some of the revengeful moods he felt inside him lately.

He waited patiently for the three Wise Men to march sedately in from the side door, their hands glued stiffly to their sides. With how little expression Anton asked the question, "Where is he that is born King of the Jews?" Hansie himself could have done so much better.

Almost fiercely Hansie swung his way to the front of the room, swaying proudly, commanding the attention of every member of his class. His mother had read to him the story, and he knew that he must be troubled and provoked in a beastly way. Throwing his shoulders back, peering down his nose with the effrontery and brassiness of the wicked ruler he was portraying, he demanded of the Wise Men to find the child, that he might worship Him also. His voice dripped with sarcasm and hypocrisy. For a moment the "Wise Men" were stunned. They looked at Fräulein Bartel, wondering if Hansie were not overdoing his part. But her sense of humor, carefully guarded beneath a look of dignity, was well under control.

Anton faced his enemy savagely. He had hoped that the teacher would take Hansie down a notch, but she was now busy getting the angels to stand up a little straighter and helping that stupid Agatha with her part. Hopefully he watched the faces of his classmates, but as usual Hansie was the hero. There was no amusement nor disrespect visible anywhere. Irmgart, her pretty face glowing, was whispering something to Hansie, something complimentary to be sure, from where she stood in the line of angels.

Then Anton got an idea. He had acted his part poorly, indeed, but it wasn't hard to imitate someone else. Standing back with the other Wise Men, his forehead puckered, he looked for his chance. It came much sooner than he expected. Fräulein Bartel took the angels outside the room to give them some last-minute instructions, so that they would come in the proper order and sing their song at just the right moment.

Throwing his shoulders back in great exaggeration, Anton raised his arm. "Go and search diligently for the young child," he rasped.

The classroom roared with laughter; it had been a perfect travesty. Hansie, now back in his seat, felt his face get red, felt his heart quicken with anger, felt shameful tears come to eyes that did not cry. Not since those days in the East Zone, when the children had made fun of his shoes, had he felt so chagrined. But shoes were a small loss beside his pride, which now lay shattered before his classmates. He did not dare look at Anton, the spoiler of all that was beautiful and wonderful in his life. How could he ever play the part of King Herod now that it had been so ridiculed by the hated Anton? He hated him—hated the half-Russian boy. Surely the half-Mennonite in him was poorly represented!

Glaring down at the hard surface of his desk, Hans did not see Fräulein Bartel enter.

"What is going on in here?" It was not often that Fräulein Bartel had to resort to such sternness.

Silence.

"Hans Penner, you look guilty. Will you please tell us what happened while I was out of the room?"

More silence. Fräulein Bartel looked perplexed. She secretly loved the spunky, vivacious boy, and his raised eyes showed tears she hadn't realized were there.

"Well, I guess we can't finish our practice until we

223

know what happened. Will you tell me, please, Irmgart?"

Still more silence.

Then Irmgart could hold out no longer. Of all the admirers of the unpredictable Hansie, she was probably the stanchest. She had not laughed with the rest of the class, but had stood electrified.

"He—Anton—made fun of Hans' part. It was most unfair."

"As soon as class is over, will Hans and Anton walk back to the *Lager* with me? We have a few things to talk over. But in the meantime we must go through this whole practice again."

Fräulein Bartel ended her mandate with finality. But it was not as simple as all that. Hansie sat, disgraced, paralyzed. How carefully he had studied with Mamma the part, how effectively he had acted it out! But he would not go through that part again!

The angels sang to the shepherds; the shepherds went to worship the child Jesus; little Mary played her part with innocent sweetness; Joseph looked lovingly down at the imaginary baby lying in its imaginary cradle. Fräulein Bartel was working hard to get enough materials to costume and set her stage, and she was accomplishing her task with extraordinary results. Finally came the scene of the Wise Men from the East, one of them a very sober and much wiser man than he had been five minutes before.

Breathlessly the class waited for Hansie's part. There was not a blond head in the whole room which did not turn to the fourth seat in the third row when the haughty King Herod was due to enter. But the seat remained occupied, and the occupant sat, his face buried in his clammy hands, with his body motionless.

There was kindness in Fräulein Bartel's voice. "You played your part so well, Hans. Hans, we're waiting."

Still Hansie did not rise. King Herod had died within him, and he was only a schoolboy, humiliated in front of his friends. Sensing his hurt and knowing his stubbornness, Fräulein Bartel proceeded with her practice, helping Rosie and Agatha and Sarah with their poems, changing her mind about how she thought the angels should stand, guiding the little Dietrich through his arduous recitation.

The day was over at last and the class dismissed. Methodically Hansie gathered up his notebook and pencil and stood, soldierlike, beside his desk. Anton looked out the window, his hands in his pockets, angry and jealous that Irmgart had taken Hansie's side. Fräulein Bartel sighed and prayed for wisdom as she gathered up her worn books and tidied the schoolroom for the regular city classes the next day. She pushed Anton out ahead of her, beckoning Hansie behind her, and the three figures headed down the dirt path toward the main street.

Hansie vowed himself to silence. He would not, he could not, confide in Fräulein Bartel in front of Anton. Instead of thinking of his sins, as Fräulein Bartel no doubt expected of him, he kept his eyes studiously on the path beneath him, twice running into little old ladies as they shuffled through the town of Gronau. His thoughts were of what he would do to Anton if he ever got a chance, dangerous thoughts, thoughts that would have shocked Mamma and Rosie. Once he saw Rosie ahead with Agatha and Irmgart, saw her look nervously, lovingly backward. He wondered if she would go to the hospital and tell Mamma what had happened. Once he stole a look at the enemy marching proudly and just as stubbornly on the other side, the safe side, of Fräulein Bartel. He waited for her to begin her lecture.

At last she started, her tired eyes resting on one and then the other, grave with a seriousness they hadn't quite expected.

"I've noticed, Anton and Hans, that you boys don't get along together very well. Don't you like each other?"

They didn't think she would come right out with it like that. Neither replied to a question so indelicately stated, so obviously true.

"Now, Hans, what is it you have against Anton? This is Christmas and we're reading about the song of the angels, 'Peace on earth, good will toward men.' That is what the Lord came for. How can you boys quarrel and hurt one another when Christ came to bring love and kindness?"

Hansie did not want to talk about love and kindness. An injustice had been committed; he would speak of love and kindness when justice had been meted out. And he could *hardly* wait for the Lord to do that for him. That was his business. Nor was he going to do it through Fräulein Bartel. He was a man. He bit his lower lip and determined to say nothing. Whatever the boy on the other side was thinking, he, too, refused to speak. Finally Fräulein Bartel gave up, ushered the lads into their quarters, and returned lamely to her own little room. She planned to pray about her problem and see what help Fräulein Siemens could give her. The steps below her seemed uglier than usual, bare except for cakes of dirt which had been dragged in by some of the feet she heard scuffling here and there in the *Lager*.

When she was safely out of the way, Hansie answered all Rosie's anxious questions with an "ugh" and hurried out to the veranda. He passed a group of other children organized in a game, passed the old grandmas, knitting contentedly and uneventfully by the late afternoon light, turned the corner around the *Klubhaus,* and spied Anton. The boy was where he knew he would be, walking aimlessly around in his own bad company. Hansie had never before fought with anyone, and he hardly knew how to go about it. But the job had to be done, and he was the one to do it.

Warily his watchful eye swept the terraces on this more lonely side of the *Klubhaus* to be sure that there would be no audience. Irmgart appeared and disappeared, and he waited patiently until he was sure that she was gone. Once his heart almost gave way as he saw the red and gold symbol on the arm of one of the MCC workers hurrying into the *Lager*. He tried to blot out from his mind the picture of that cross and handshake which his mother had told him meant love and peace, or something like that. Those things did not fall in the realm of justice, of meting out punishment to the wicked.

At last the coast was clear. No Irmgarts, no MCC workers, no parents or children to see him.

Half an hour later, as he lay sobbing and bloody on his cot with Rosie bending over him, he wondered where they had all come from and how they had gotten there so quickly. Round and round in his head went the crowd that had gathered: grandmas, mammas, babies, schoolmates, Irmgart, and MCC workers. He wept now unashamedly, wondering how Anton's head felt (he hadn't meant to knock him so hard), and wondering if his own nose would ever be the same again. As insistent as the beating sound in his brain was the fear of what this would do to Mamma, lying quietly in the hospital across the yard from him. Over and over the words went through his mind, spoken firmly to him by the *Hausvater*:

"We will not tell your mother; you will have to do that yourself."

29

THE DAY HAD NOT BEEN so eventful for Maria. Confined
by doctor's orders, she lay resting, hopeful that she
would pass the next physical examination for entrance
into Canada, the land of her dreams. The only window
in the room faced west, westward toward the land of
promise, the somewhere that refugees were always going.
Indeed, the sky was beautiful at this moment, for the sun
was almost down and God had turned His lights very
low.

At this time of the evening the two villas nearest the
hospital dejected Maria. The closest one to the *lager*
must have been very lovely before the blitz, but now, except for the framework and a few supporting walls, it had
been reduced to a pile of debris. Next to this unsightly
building stood another one, owned by a wealthy citizen
and completely undamaged, seemingly turning an unsym-
pathetic back to its neighbor in need.

The one shall be taken and the other left, Maria
thought to herself, as she mused on how that Scripture,
taken of course from its context, seemed to be fulfilled
in her life and the life of all children of war. Who could
say why fate struck as it did, often leaving the guilty and
taking the lives of the guiltless? Surely when Christ returned to earth, His taking one and leaving another
would be in complete fairness to all.

The evening dragged on and the supper hour arrived
at last. Fräulein Sawatzky came in cautiously, careful

not to spill the steaming soup which she carried on her tray. She was the muscular type of girl, the kind who balanced a tray with ease. One could see that she was used to harder work than a girl her age should have known. Yet her eyes twinkled and her face wore a smile.

"Surprise tonight," she announced gaily, resting a tray with soup and bun on the knees of the closest patient. "White rolls for the hospital dwellers."

Then she turned on a dim light in the corner close to where Frau Loewen was trying to read and hurried from the room to bring up supper for the others.

By this time it was dark outside, and the little light in the corner of the room cast weird reflections on the wall. Frau Loewen, sitting in her wheel chair, made an interesting portrait in the lamplight, holding her Bible in her one good hand. Maria looked pityingly at her other limp one, hanging in its useless position. She noticed the shadow of Frau Loewen's arm looming large on the wall behind her, like a gentleman's cane or a long-necked swan. The door opened again, and the crippled saint laid aside her Bible to take the tray on her lap, her eyes moist with appreciation at the extra treat of the evening.

Lamplight hours were lovely hours. Eating in silence, Maria thought of what would be going on in the only home she knew, the little blanketed cell of life that was her own. For children like hers the evening hours were satisfying times of being together, of reviewing the school joys of the day, of a brief recitation of a lesson well learned. And particularly in this Christmas season, the walls of every little room would hear the Christmas recitations, repeated again and again until perfect. There would be correction, but the eyes of the little ones would sparkle and the parents would listen with pride.

Yes, lamplight hour was an impressive hour. For Maria it was a period of devotion, thanksgiving for another day of safety, a time to gather courage, a time to offer prayer. Soon after supper, the door would swing open and her young ones would come in for their evening visit, Hansie usually blustering in, Rosie tiptoeing shyly.

"Isn't it about time your children come to see you?" Frau Loewen asked at length, when she had finished her supper and the nurse was gathering the empty dishes on her tray.

"They are rather late, aren't they? What time is it, Fräulein Sawatzky?"

"It's 7:30, Frau Penner, but maybe I should—"

"Should what? Is—is anything wrong with the children?"

"I didn't mean to frighten you. It isn't really that bad. Only, Hansie got himself in trouble this evening. Nothing serious or anything like that. But if he shouldn't come, he'll come tomorrow."

Emma Sawatzky repented that she had mentioned Hansie's predicament when she looked at Maria's face.

"Really, Frau Penner, it wasn't serious—only a child's fight. But Hansie is a bit in disgrace with the *Hausvater*, if you know what I mean. Oh, he'll show up sooner or later, and then let him tell you. Please don't worry about it."

Perhaps one could feel that way if it were not your own child, Maria thought. *Just what had Hansie done?* It seemed hours before the door opened. And then only Rosie slipped in.

231

Rosie knew that the question would be forthcoming and had all the way up the steps been formulating a reply. Yet when her mother asked her where Hansie was, the answer seemed lodged in her throat.

"He—oh, Mamma, Hansie's in trouble. The nurse is bathing his eye downstairs. He'll come up pretty soon." She looked distressed.

"Don't you worry about it, Rosie. We'll let Hansie explain when he comes. How was school today?"

"Mamma, my part is practically learned. Do you want to hear it?" Rosie brightened and stood very straight, not failing to notice the admiration in the eyes of the other women. She half turned toward Frau Loewen, glancing from her to Maria.

"It is a very sad poem, isn't it, Mother?" she commented to relieve the quietness that seemed to follow. The older women were wiping their eyes and Maria, instead of giving her usual words of encouragement, was staring at Rosie in wonder, unable to see how a child could put so much meaning into a poem.

"You said it beautifully," Maria responded. "It is indeed sad, but very true. I'm glad it has such a nice ending, aren't you?"

Hansie seemed to have chosen the psychological moment to make his entrance. Like a crippled and badly frightened fawn, he hesitated at the door, his guilty, bruised face peering cautiously around the corner. Then he walked over to his mother's bed, in a businesslike way, avoiding the eyes of the nonfamily members in the room. How he wished they were not there! It was hard enough as it was.

Seeing her prodigal, Maria instinctively propped herself up a little higher, dismissing Rosie to some finishing work on her poem.

"Hello, Hansie."

A long silence followed, in which all the stubbornness in Hansie seemed to be showing itself, making more bristly the contrary tufts of hair on the top of his head, making his arms stiff and his back erect. Only a quiver of his lip betrayed his feeling. Maria loved him in his guilt more passionately than she had ever loved him on one of his "good" days.

"Hansie, I don't know what it is, but something's wrong. Come here, Son," she murmured, motioning him to come into whispering range of her.

"How did you know?" Gladly he snuggled up to his mother, who lay so familiar and warm beneath the sheet. She was his oasis in an unfriendly world, the one person who understood.

"Someone told me you were in trouble with the *Hausvater*. Tell me about it. I won't scold you."

Hansie looked about him to be sure that no one was hearing. He was tired of outside interference. He noticed that Fräulein Sawatzky had come in to help Frau Loewen to bed, that the old woman next to Mamma had her eyes closed and looked about as interested in his problems as a corpse. He slipped over on the other side of the bed and pulled up a chair.

"It was Anton, Mamma."

"You and Anton don't get along very well, do you, Hansie?"

She thought she would make it easier for him. The close-up view showed little injuries on his face that she

233

hadn't noticed when he came into the room—a cut on the nose, another on the lip.

"He made fun of my part, Mamma, in front of the whole class. I could never give it again. I shall never give it again. They—they all liked it when I said it, but when the teacher was out of the room and all the students just waiting for her to come back in, he suddenly got up and mocked my part—and—"

He had been talking rapidly. Suddenly he hid his face to conceal his tears as he had done that time when Hans, Big Hans, had knelt so tenderly beside him because of the shoes. She couldn't help thinking that in both cases it was hurt pride. Both her Hanses were *so* proud.

"Did the rest of the children approve of Anton's fun?"

"They—they really laughed, Mamma."

"But that didn't ruin your part, Hansie. Children like to laugh; they have probably forgotten all about it by this time."

His voice was bitter. "It will never be the same. Whenever they hear it they won't listen as they did before. They will hide their faces and giggle, because he mocked everything I did. His own part was rotten, Mamma. He was jealous."

A long silence followed. Maria knew that the hardest part of the story for Hans was not the injustice done but what he had done about it.

"The story isn't finished, Hansie. You must tell it all. Otherwise, you will not be able to sleep." She looked at his troubled face, his accordion-pleated forehead.

"Tell me how you got the black eye and the cuts."

He opened his mouth, then closed it again. Finally,

concentrating on a dim light in the street below, he began.

"I have to tell the whole story first. As I said, Anton makes fun of my part, then the teacher comes in and wants to know what happened; so she asks Irmgart and Irmgart takes my side and tells her. She (the teacher) makes us both walk home with her from school, and oh, yes, I forgot, she makes everybody do the whole play over and when my part comes I just can't get up, Mamma. I shall never give that part again!"

"So they went on without you?"

"First I just felt awful, as if I could never face any of them again. Then I began to get mad, Mamma, madder than I ever have at that Anton, so mad, Mamma, I could—"

A look at his mother's face stopped him. He changed what he had been planning to say.

"He's Russian, Mamma, that's what makes him so mean. It's the Russians who make everybody unhappy. That's why you're crying, Mamma, that's why you always cry, because of the Russians. That's why everybody's always scared and why old Frau Arndt can't sleep at nights. That's why we aren't with Papa right now, or Tante Anni, or Grandma and Grandpa Maier."

"Hansie!"

"When I finally grow up, Mamma, and we go to Canada, and I get rich, I'm going to join some army and come back." He had never voiced anything so strongly, and he did it on a dare to himself. "I hate Russians; I hate Anton."

Maria stared at Hansie in unbelief.

"Tell me the rest of the story before we talk about the Russians. How did you get those scars on your face?"

"When we got back to the *Lager*, Anton and Fräulein Bartel and me, she went to her room upstairs and I just went to ours for a minute. Then I went out where Anton always plays. When everybody was out of sight I punished the Russian in him, that's all. I beat him up and taught him a lesson. But one of the children saw us and told everybody and—"

Here he broke down again.

"So everyone saw the fight then, and the *Hausvater* came out to stop you?"

"Yes, Herr Toews stopped us."

"How badly is Anton hurt?"

"Does it matter?"

"Hans, it matters very much."

Hansie sat in silence a long time before he tried to speak. Then Emma Sawatzky came in again on the pretense of seeing that everyone was comfortable.

"Fräulein Sawatzky, is Anton Braun badly hurt?"

The nurse gave a children-will-be-children look and answered, "Oh, he'll live, just a slight cut on the head where he fell when Hansie knocked him over. He had a few rebounds on Hansie, I believe, before Herr Toews got to the scene and stopped things."

She stole another glance at the boy, hurrying from the room to visit the next of her charges.

"It wasn't like that at all, Mamma. He hit me on the chin first and when I tried to push him away, he fell over a stone and—"

"But you started the whole thing, Son. You said you did."

"I know it."

"Hansie, you say that Anton is Russian and that Russians are the cause of all the wrongs in the world. I didn't realize that you have been thinking such revengeful thoughts. Do you remember how, just before the doctor sent me over to the hospital, I called on Anton's mother? You didn't like it very well, did you?"

"I still don't know why you did it. None of the other women in the camp would have."

"Hansie, Anton's mother is a very lonely woman. Anton's father is a Mennonite, but he married a lady who doesn't know very much about us and has never learned our language nor much about our beliefs. She is no bad woman, but she knows the women in camp don't like her and that makes her shy and causes her to do some things other people don't like. How would you feel if no one liked you? Why Hansie, even when Anton did you a small injustice, nothing compared to the way Frau Braun has been treated, you got offended. Do you know what she did, Hansie, when I visited her? She broke down and cried because someone was interested. She told me all her troubles, all about her home in Russia, about how she happened to marry Anton's father. She told me that the reason Anton is often so poorly behaved is because he feels badly, too, that the other children don't like him. Can't you see how you would treat people if you knew they hated you?"

"Is that why he is always making fun of someone and acting so nasty?"

"That's the reason. I've been wanting to talk to you about him for a long time and see if you might try to

237

help him, but you've never even let me get on the subject.

"And, Hansie, did you know that I wouldn't be here today, had not a Russian woman saved my life? It wasn't long after our home was torn up that we were stranded in a little town and I was terribly sick. I've told you the story before, how an old Russian mother took me into her home and with great love and kindness nursed me back to health.

"It is true that the Communist party is cruel and godless, but that does not mean the peoples of Russia are by nature bad. In fact, most of the Russians I have known were tender-hearted, easily moved to tears, hospitable, and fond of singing and other music. They, too, are afraid of the Communist party. I think we should pray for them, Hans

"You see, Son, there are both good and bad people in every country, though often the governments are corrupt. When we came into Germany, we thought, How good to get out of Russia, but soon we met selfish Germans and soon we learned that Nazi officials had done heartless things during the war. And then, Hansie, when we got into the western zones of Germany, we learned that not everything is done according to Christian standards here. I think it will be that way wherever we go.

"War, Son, is wicked wherever it is and whoever does it. Nothing can make it right. Innocent men, women, and children are killed on both sides. The Bible teaches us to love people instead of hating them. That's why our dear friends from America have come over to help us. They share their goods with everyone, regardless of nationality, race, or creed, 'in the name of Christ.' "

238

She laid her hand on his.

"That's why Jesus came into the world as a tiny baby, to spread peace and good will among all peoples everywhere, Hans."

Hansie sat and stared at the precious hump in the sheet that was his mother. He thought about Christmas and about the shepherds and the Wise Men. He remembered how wonderful the story had sounded to him from his mother's lips, how it was this year for the first time that he felt he really understood.

They shared a moment of quiet thought.

"You've heard me tell it to others, Hansie, how unhappy I was before Pastor Jung showed me that Jesus Christ was the answer to my despair and loneliness. Of course, I knew about Christ before, but I had never actually accepted His love into my life. But that is something each one of us must do, accept that love for himself."

"But I'm too young to be a Christian, if that's what you mean, Mamma."

"It seems to me that boys who are old enough to have hate and revenge in their hearts are also old enough to accept the love of God."

He hadn't thought of it that way before.

"I'd have to tell Anton I'm sorry, wouldn't I?" he asked huskily.

"What do you think, Hansie?"

"That would be hard."

She did not urge him, for it would have been as useless to try pushing Hansie into the kingdom as it was to shove the beloved Big Hans in. They were men who had to make up their minds for themselves.

Suddenly the awkward stillness was broken by music in the hall, sweet, well-blended women's voices floating soothingly to the hearts of the patients. It was the nurses on one of their surprise singing tours, huddled together over a few paper-backed books. Tonight they sang "Silent Night, Holy Night," vibrant with meaning in the original German in which it was written.

All of this was too much for Hansie. When he returned to the *Lager* a short time later, the load of hate had given way to an inward peace. Yet two assignments lay heavy on his heart, both of them hard ones. For how difficult it would be to play the part of the wicked King Herod now, and how hard it would be to make that apology!

30

A GENTLE SNOW dropped lightly on the cobblestone street in front of the railway station in Gronau. Framed in the doorway, the snow-sprinkled town was an enchanting sight, luring Hans to explore its moonlit charm. The ticket agent, having informed him where he would find the Mennonites, watched with friendly interest as he adjusted his pack and picked up the wooden suitcase he had made for the trip.

"Come a long way?"

Hans looked at him quickly, suspiciously. Then, when he saw courteous eyes peering through heavy glasses, he was ashamed. He ventured a smile.

"A long way, sir."

"Well, a blessed Christmas to you."

Hans stopped and turned sharply around, setting his suitcase on the floor.

"That's right, this is Christmas Eve, isn't it?"

Then, seeing the amazed look on the face of the other man, Hans hastened to add, "Of course, I knew it was almost Christmas, but I've had so much on my mind I didn't realize it was already Christmas Eve."

The agent smiled. "That's all right," he said, sensing Hans' embarrassment. "A blessed Christmas to you."

Hans headed for the door.

"Let's see, you said the camp is four blocks south and two blocks west? Thank you. A blessed Christmas to you, too."

He walked out, wondering if it was because he had not yet gotten his land legs that he felt so wobbly, or perhaps that he had had only one meal all day, or that thoughts of Christmas were thoughts of home and Maria and the children. How would they be spending Christmas? Even with his trek behind him, arriving at a place where there were others of his kind, Hans could not feel truly cheered when he remembered his family. No, his heart would never be light, knowing that they were hungry, cold, and overworked. There was only one thing that brought him hope since that awful night almost two years ago, and he reached his hand into his pocket to be sure the little volume was still there. In recent months it had become more prized than his identification card. Two years: Maria would be almost forty, Hans twelve, Rosie ten. If Lenie had lived, she would be—.

Hans quickened his pace. He couldn't stand to go on thinking; he might remember that last Christmas they had spent together, materially poor, but *together*. He paused and blew his nose on the tattered handkerchief he had laundered for the trip.

The street was not well lit, but through the windows of the homes along the way he saw festivity, family life at its best. There was laughter and fun, though Hans knew that there were no delicious pastries nor fine gifts to be had this Christmas. One window radiated so much joy that he stopped to rest a moment. Although he knew he shouldn't do it, he tiptoed as close as he dared and gazed through the pane, noticing that the family sat circled around the father, listening contentedly to the reading of the sacred story.

Churches in the town were ringing their bells, the peals

spelling out long-forgotten melodies. Farther in the city the street lights made glistening the snow beneath Hans' feet, and here and there a stranger hurried home. No one wanted to be on the streets on this night of the year. Except for an occasional street light, Gronau was like a city deserted, its rambling, crooked business section dark and lonely. At last Hans arrived at the main street and turned the corner as he had been directed. His steps became lighter as he realized how near he was to his destination.

Would the people there really care? Was there genuine love awaiting him? Sometimes, many times, he felt that no man cared for his soul. But this was Christmas Eve—

Then there was the sign, only a simple wooden one to be sure, but bearing the welcome words, *Mennonite Central Committee of the United States and Canada,* in bold, black letters. He passed through the heavy iron gate and slowly mounted the few steps to the porch. Everything was quiet, as though no one was there. Inside the entrance was a light, and at his knock a young man came to the door.

Hans stepped inside. That the chap was a Mennonite he was sure; in *Platt* Hans told him about the long road behind him and his hopes for admission to camp. He noticed as he talked that on one arm the boy, certainly no older than eighteen, bore a simple band, "MCC Guard," and that the other sleeve of his drab coat was tucked neatly in his pocket. The absurdity of a gunless guard with only one arm later amused Hans, but at the moment his own need for companionship and friendly advice blinded him to such insignificant details.

"I can't admit you to camp, or anything like that, but you can hang around until the director or camp leader comes back from the program," the boy suggested in an accommodating manner.

"Everybody around here is at the Christmas program. I wish I could have gone myself, but someone had to stick around, and I will get my chance tomorrow. Say, you're probably hungry."

Hans got up from the staircase where he had sat down, suddenly realizing how weak he really was. But he was ashamed that he showed it.

"Look, Penner—that's what you said your name is?— we got extra rations from the government for Christmas. Take this. I had supper."

The guard reached his good hand into his right pocket and pulled out a chocolate bar.

"Are—are you sure?" The generous offer was almost too much for Hans.

Friends, friends again. While he ate his chocolate, the first he had had for six years, he told the young Heinrich Hildebrandt about his border crossing, about how he heard of the camp in the first place.

The boy listened with more than casual interest. Though the stories were so often the same, each had its own variation of suspense and danger, of escapades and miracles. His own day of miracles was not so far behind that Heinrich could not understand every emotion that shook the body of the older man across from him. He tried to guess how old Hans was, and judged that he was not far beyond the thirties, though he had prematurely gray hair.

"Say, listen," Heinrich said at length, when Hans had

finished his chocolate bar and the condensed story of the past years of his life, "by this time the program will have barely started, probably won't be any further than the devotional service. Would you be interested in going? It would do you good. After all, this is Christmas Eve."

"Yes, I hardly realized it until the station agent wished me a blessed Christmas."

"Did you have a family?" Heinrich had no sooner asked the question than he regretted it. Of course, a man as old as Hans would have a family. How could he have been so tactless as to bring up this subject? Accepting the nod as an answer, Heinrich hastily began giving Hans instructions for finding the old theater where the services were being held.

When Hans arrived at the theater, only a few blocks from the camp itself and back in the same direction from which he had come, the snow was swirling and the wind almost bitter. He pulled his collar around his neck and walked briskly to the door. Then he paused, bowing his head as he heard the song, *"So nimm denn meine Haende"* ("Take Thou my hand, O Father, and lead Thou me, until my journey endeth, eternally. Alone I will not wander one single day; be Thou my true Companion and with me stay").

Was he dreaming? Were these the voices of his own brethren? Were they doing this unhindered? Was this Heaven? His wobbly legs and his still-empty stomach assured him that he hadn't reached Heaven yet. Inconspicuously he stumbled to the back row, sighing at the beauty of the two large Christmas trees in front, decorated with candles which gave the only light to the impressive scene that followed.

Hans looked about him, speaking to his neighbor in *Platt,* discovering that there were probably six hundred people in the large room. Then the program began, as three little boys in succession recited loud and clear, their hands stiffened to their sides, their shoulders thrown back. When their pieces, lovely little poems about Christmas and God and home, were finished, they bowed politely, some of them very low indeed, and hurried off the platform. One fellow got quite mixed up and bowed at the wrong time, an effect so comical that the boys and the audience could not help laughing. Small girls, too, gave their pieces distinctly, uninhibited by stage fright, and afterward remembered their graceful curtsies.

When about twenty minutes of these recitations were concluded, the schoolteacher announced that the whole congregation would sing "Silent Night." Hans could not sing, but in the trembling loveliness of that moment, he thought he felt the presence of the Christ child with him and the noise of the angel wings above. The songs by the young people, who stood to the right of the platform, were likewise sweet, and, it seemed to Hans, celestial in quality.

After the singing had ended, Hans noticed that there was a great deal of commotion on the platform, scenes being set up, costumed children slipping here and there to get into their proper places. He leaned forward, cupping his chin in his hand, watching the excited movements of the children. Where had they gotten those original costumes? No doubt the robes the shepherds were wearing were old blankets salvaged from possessions the refugees had dragged along with them from the East. One little angel almost tripped with her candle.

Hans shifted uneasily in his chair. He wished he were not sitting so far back. A fellow older than his Hansie reminded him of the boy, standing proudly on the platform as King Herod and blaring out with dramatic cruelty the words of the wicked king. Of course, Hansie had a voice almost like a girl, while this fellow had a coarse, uncertain voice already deepening. But it was his mannerisms under the heavy costume that reminded the lonely man so much of his lost son.

The play lasted about fifteen minutes, and was followed by several other selections from the choir. Hans leaned back and drank in the words. Physical hunger had long since given way to the need of his soul, and he was being fed in a way that he had not dreamed. He was sorry when the voices ceased singing, though the poems the children gave were touching and beautiful. Closing his eyes, he listened as three schoolgirls took turns reciting verses in a homespun poem, full of the deep longings of a refugee.

All of a sudden Hans opened his eyes with a start. *That voice!* Not quite like hers, yet almost. One freckle-faced (he was sure she had freckles) little girl with long, auburn braids had stepped out from among the others to say her verse. The way she pronounced her words, the slow, lovely rhythm of her voice, brought Hans to his feet. Pushing his way up the aisle, he strained to see her better. It was Rosie! Of that he was sure! He dropped into an empty seat, leaning forward to hear the words,

> For though our homes may seem so far away,
> And though there's sorrow in our lives each day,
> The peace of Christmastime is here to stay.

247

Then he bowed his head and wept, cried like the women in the row behind him who were moved by the sentiment of the poem. Perhaps they thought it strange that a man should be so touched by the verse, but they were too engrossed in their own thoughts to pay much attention to him.

Hans began looking for Maria, at the same time trying to relocate the boy he had thought sounded like his Hansie. He could see only anonymous heads in the dim candlelight, and felt he would go mad if he didn't find them. Rosie had sat down on the very front row and going to her would have completely upset the program. She would have fainted or screamed, he was sure.

His search, however, was suddenly interrupted by a change in the program; apparently the school children had finished their part of the evening's worship. Two men walked soberly to the platform, Bibles in hand. Hans' heart raced within him as the older minister read a portion of Scripture and as the younger called for some moments of silent prayer. The choir sang one more selection, beautiful but seemingly never-ending. Hans bounded for the door, unmindful that a benediction was being pronounced.

He stood just outside the entrance, his heart beating wildly. Then the door flew open and dozens of children poured forth from the building, some of them waiting for their mothers, some walking in groups toward the MCC house. For a moment he thought he was going to be lost in the push of the crowd. But he could not allow that to happen. He stood his ground, scanning every face that came out of the building.

And then he saw them, coming on the opposite side

of the entrance from where he stood. He cut through the crowd and stationed himself several feet ahead of them. Hansie and Rosie went by, but Maria walked into his arms.

"Oh, excuse me," she apologized, her face crimson. Then she looked at him again. He drew her closer and kissed her, right there in full sight of everyone, unconscious that anyone else was around.

"You came, you really came!" Maria cried when she could talk. "I wanted so much to believe it."

It was then that the children missed their mother and retraced their steps to find her. And the crying, exclamations, and kissing began all over again, with no one ashamed of his tears.

The walk back to camp which the four of them made together, hand in hand, everyone talking at once, would have been quite a spectacle had they not chosen a long, out-of-the-way route. Only after they sat whispering in their little room, long after all others had gone to bed, did everything really begin to make sense.

"You see," Big Hans was saying, as he tried to embrace them all at once, "first I found God, and then I found you. I had given you up altogether, after what Frau Schmidt told me. I had gotten to the end of myself when I began to read that Testament which was really meant for you, Maria."

"Do you mean, Dear, that if you had never lost us, you probably would never have found God?"

"I'm afraid I wouldn't have. I guess it wasn't that I couldn't believe, but I really was too stubborn to want to believe. But how I deserved to find you again, that I can't understand. I guess I never will."

They talked on and on, Hans describing his life in Berlin, his frightening border crossing, his wearisome experiences at Kassel. He told of the Martens and the beginning of his new life in God. Then Maria, Hansie, and Rosie interrupted each other in bringing Hans up to date on their adventures along the way. They ended by telling about Maria's recent physical examination and the disappointing news that Canada had refused them entrance again on the basis of her ill health.

But going to Paraguay would no longer be a disappointment now that Big Hans was here. For where one lived was really unimportant, when people could be together, happy in each other's love. What joy it would be to pioneer with a partner like Hans!

Rosie had finally dropped off to sleep, her long braids buried in her father's lap. Maria, seated between the two Hanses, was once more startled at the striking resemblance of strong facial lines and stubborn expression, visible against the low flicker of candlelight. But now both faces wore a new expression, the evidence of an enduring peace, the kind of peace on earth that begins in the hearts of men.

Indeed, it was the only kind of peace Maria's battered world would ever know.

Glossary of German Words

Note: The German *r* should be rolled slightly.

Bahnhof (bän′ hōf)—railroad station

Bahnhöfen (bän hȯif′ ən)—railroad stations

Evangelische (ā fän gel′ ish ā)—Lutheran or Reformed; Protestant churches in Germany

Frau (frȯ)—Mrs.

Fräulein (frȯi līn′)—Miss, or young lady, abbreviated *Frl.*

Gut (güt)—large estate

Guten Appetit (güt′ ən äp′ e tēt)—a common greeting at mealtime, literally, "good appetite"

Hausvater (hȯs′ fät ər)—house father, responsible for supervision of camp life in a *Lager.*

Herr (her)—Mr.

Klompen (kläm′ pən)—wooden shoes

Klubhaus (kləb′ hȯs′)—clubhouse. In Gronau, an auditorium-sized building requisitioned by MCC for living quarters for refugees. Also referred to as *Lager.*

Lager (läg′ er)—camp building

Lagerleiter (läg′ er līt′ er)—camp leader

Plattdeutsch (plät′ dȯich) or **Platt** (plät)—Low German dialect

SS, abbreviation for **Schutzstaffel** (shüts′ shtäf əl)—Nazi Storm Troopers, an elite force in Hitler's army

251

Schul-Ranzen (shül′ rän′ sən)—schoolbag
Strasse (shträ′ sā)—street
Tante (tän′ tā)—aunt
Verschleppt (fər shlept′)—literally, "dragged away," as forced labor into the northern lands of Siberia
Wehrmacht (ver′ mäkht)—literally, "war machine," the German army

ACKNOWLEDGMENTS

I wish to express my appreciation to the many friends who encouraged me in writing this story and who helped me in various ways. Life stories, carefully written out by former refugees now settled in Canada and Paraguay, were a great help. I am also indebted to German friends and recent immigrants to this country who answered questions for me and who read my manuscript. Among those who offered valuable suggestions I wish to especially thank the following people: Peter J. Dyck, former administrator in the MCC refugee program; A. Grace Wenger, Eastern Mennonite College, Harrisonburg, Virginia; Melvin Gingerich, Ph.D., Goshen College, Goshen, Indiana; and Miriam Sieber Lind, Scottdale, Pennsylvania.